MATHEMATICS POWER LEARNING FOR CHILDREN

ACTIVATING THE CONTEXTUAL LEARNER

BOOK ONE

Everard Barrett

CONTEXTUAL MATHEMATICS TEACHING METHODOLOGY

Professor B Enterprises, Inc.
P. O. Box 2079
Duluth, GA 30096
www.profb.com

FIFTH EDITION REVISED

MATHEMATICS POWER LEARNING FOR CHILDREN
ACTIVATING THE CONTEXTUAL LEARNER

Copyrights and acknowledgments

Editor
Everard Barrett

Production Manager
Veda Barrett

Cover Art
Charles J. Berger

Publisher
Professor B Enterprises, Inc.
P. O. Box 2079
Duluth, GA 30096
www.profb.com

Published in the United States by Professor B Enterprises, Inc. Portions of this text were previously published under the following titles:

FIFTH EDITION REVISED

ISBN 1-883324-01-7

Library of Congress Catalog Card Number: 93-92702

Printed in the United States of America

To Him that is able to keep me from falling.

ABOUT THE AUTHOR

Everard Barrett has been an Associate Professor in the Mathematics Department, State University of New York, College at Old Westbury since 1971 and is the president of Professor B Enterprises, Inc. From 1962 to 1971, he taught junior and senior high school mathematics in Brooklyn, New York.

He is the originator of the Contextual Mathematics Teaching Methodology and has conducted numerous interventions in public schools within twelve states of the U.S. since 1973. Results, as substantiated by many statistical analyses, have been consistently strong. Over and over again, he has moved his projects through the cycle of implementation, teachers' feedback, statistical evaluation, and revision.

In June 1976, after three years of experimental work in the Theodore Roosevelt Elementary School, Roosevelt, New York, he broke new educational ground by enabling fifth and sixth grade classes to out-perform (by a wide margin) their ninth grade counterparts on an examination traditionally reserved for the brightest ninth graders (The New York State Ninth Year Algebra Regents Examination) throughout the state. This was subsequently repeated (on two occasions) in P.S. 44, an elementary school within Central Bedford Stuyvesant, Brooklyn, New York.

Professor Barrett was commissioned to a UNESCO mission in mathematics education in St. Lucia, Grenada, and Jamaica at the request of their governments in 1980. Following the World Conference on Education for All in Jomtien, Thailand during March, 1990, he was invited to present his methodology at the first seminar held by the United Nations Development Program (UNDP) in its search for "fresh, theoretically grounded methodologies for addressing fundamental educational requirements" (such as those identified at Jomtien). The one and one-half day session, on "Innovative Approaches to Meeting Basic Learning Needs," was convened at UNDP Headquarters, New York, in January, 1991. Professor Barrett was one of four presenters. Participants were educational specialists and program staff from international agencies such as UNDP, UNESCO, the World Bank, UNICEF, bilateral agencies and institutes. The director of UNESCO's International Institute for Educational Planning (IIEP) attended throughout the duration of the seminar.

The directors of IIEP and UNDP were sufficiently impressed with his methodology to refer him to the Chief of the Regional Bureau for Latin America and the Caribbean, for the purpose of initiating a UNDP-sponsored project in Jamaica, W.I.

The pilot phase of the Project was completed during Summer, 1992. After receiving training in Professor Barrett's methodology, sixteen mathematics lecturers from local teachers' colleges enabled 94% of 265 practicing primary teachers to pass a qualifying Primary Mathematics Examination, which the vast majority of them had failed repeatedly. The teachers received instruction from the lecturers for five days per week, through five weeks. The highest passing rate ever achieved previously (since 1981), by a similar population of primary teachers under the same circumstances, was only 20%. In fact, the highest passing rate ever achieved previously by a population of mixed abilities was 60%.

This impressive performance in the summer pilot has earned Professor Barrett an extension of the Project for two years. As this intervention continues, the remaining population of practicing teachers unqualified to teach mathematics will be reduced to an insignificantly small number. A national problem will have been solved.

TABLE OF CONTENTS

PREFACE

We have been firmly committed to the concept that successful pedagogy for mathematical competence in young learners can only evolve from large concentrations of time, energy, and dedication in elementary classrooms. On a yearly basis, since 1973, we have gone, full cycle, from intensive implementation and practice of the methodology, to thorough reflection upon its impact (supplemented by teachers' feedback), and then to meticulous revision.

Consequently, we have paid our dues, and our efforts have been rewarded with the development of an original pedagogy and program which guarantees accelerated learning of mathematics to virtually all children.

In order to establish credibility for our claim that virtually all children can learn mathematics successfully, we have accumulated, through these years, a huge quantity of statistical analyses. All of them show enormous growth in mathematical achievement, over relatively short periods of time, in schools which span the socio-economic spectrum. Over and over again, mean grade equivalent scores in participating elementary schools have grown from 1.5 to 3 years per year of instruction, after the first five to eight months of staff development in our methodology. Through the past twenty years, we have consistently enabled teachers to deliver mental, rapid-response knowledge of the higher addition and subtraction facts to first graders (and multiplication facts, up to five times, in some instances); as well as long division (with three-place divisors and six-place dividends) to second graders. In fact, ours is the only intervention, nationwide, which has enabled fifth and sixth grade classes, from the very lowest of socio-economic environments, to perform competently on the same exam in Algebra I, traditionally reserved for the brightest ninth graders throughout the state. This was done on three different occasions (in different school years).

How did all this happen? What were the compelling awarenesses which so effectively transformed the teachers' perspectives on the teaching of mathematics and, consequently, their pedagogical strategies and techniques in their own classrooms?

The philosophical and psychological foundations of our methodology are presented in the following reference:

> Barrett, E. (1992). "Teaching Mathematics through Context: Unleashing the Power of the Contextual Learner." In R. Tobias, ed., Nurturing At-Risk Youth in Math and Science. Bloomington, IN: National Educational Service.

However, we may briefly state here that our methodology stimulates the learning of mathematics by activating the same cognitive means by which children learn and retain stories: the ability to assimilate contextually related information. Virtually all children are competent contextual learners as demonstrated, not only by the learning of stories, but by the early mastery of their native language as well. At the core of the methodology is the awareness that mathematics is best retained by reconstruction rather than memorization. Consequently, it defines the antithesis of rote, and was created to eliminate rote learning (greatest source of remediation) from mathematics education forever.

Traditional paradigms in mathematics education suggest that the source of students' competence in this subject matter is a special "giftedness."

Our program presents a paradigm shift to the degree that:

1. at the foundation of the methodology is the understanding that the real gift for learning mathematics is the same one we used so successfully to learn language and stories before going to school (hence all learners are gifted by our Creator with the capacity to learn mathematics);
2. the methodology makes it very difficult for children to avoid learning mathematics, in contrast to the common notion that it is difficult for them to learn it;
3. accelerated development (by virtually all learners) is the inevitable outcome when the same pre-school competence for learning language and stories is activated for the learning of mathematics; and
4. accelerated learning, as achieved through the activation of the competent contextual learner in virtually all human beings, is a very enjoyable experience, in contrast to the "pushing" children experience when acceleration is attempted via traditional methodologies.

The application of the methodology to the teaching of primary and elementary mathematics is presented in Books I, II, and III: *Mathematics Power Learning for Children*.

If you are a parent or teacher, we believe you will be very surprised at the extent to which arithmetic has been presented as a sequential, developmental flow of related information in these books. Even if you can do arithmetic well, you may not have realized that it could actually make sense. As you read, you will experience the contextually related flow of concepts and skills in your mind. Consequently, your learning of the mathematics will become as certain as the learning of a story. You will discover that you can, simultaneously, learn the subject matter in these books and learn how to teach it to your children, if you are a parent; or to your students, if you are a teacher. You will now be able to provide meaningful explanations to those whose mathematical development you are in a position to influence.

It was by means of this methodology that so many "math-anxious" elementary teachers, over the years, learned the subject matter of arithmetic and Algebra I simultaneously as they learned to teach it. In fact, the vast majority of them now enjoy teaching mathematics due to their surprise discovery of its meanings. The strength of our statistical analyses provides effective testimony to the success of their efforts, and to the power of this methodology in the teaching and learning of mathematics.

We are confident that the pedagogical strategies and techniques in our three books represent a very significant breakthrough in mathematics education.

Everard Barrett

THE UNISON RESPONSE ACTIVITY

Frequently throughout our three texts, we request that you engage learners in **vocal**, rapid response, unisonous activities. The purpose of these activities is to speed up some cognitive way of knowing, which is the foundation upon which a considerable amount of knowledge is built.

One of your most important objectives, as you move learners through our "focus and concentration" activities, is a **strong, confident, unison response**.

When this happens, it is time to challenge **some individuals** (particularly the most reluctant participants) to answer by themselves, as you move them through four or five questions.

Be sure that no learner even attempts to help any individual you call on.

After achieving the confident unison responses, it is quite appropriate to vary between group and individual participation.

Learners will begin to understand that "unison time" is when they must "get ready," since they are expecting you to check on them individually.

While you are engaging them in the "rapid-fire" exercises, **keep your eyes fixed on the learners** to ensure that

1. they are **all** staring at the chart (or blackboard).
2. they are **all** responding.

The rapid-response exercises are to be moved along as quickly as the learners' responses will permit. Neither move so quickly as to overwhelm them, nor so slowly as to bore them. Find the right pace.

Speed makes it a game in which you can challenge them with, "Let's see who will win, you or me?" or "Let's see if I can catch you."

On the many occasions you will be engaging learners in the rapid-response exercises, you are to **"cut" the activity at the peak of excitement**. You will find them highly motivated to resume the challenge on subsequent days.

Throughout our twenty years of intense and sustained "hands on" staff development interventions, we have confirmed, over and over again, the power of this strategy. Your requirement that **every learner** must simultaneously vocalize the response, virtually guarantees that each participant will carefully monitor himself or herself, since no one wants his or her voice to say the wrong answer. Vocalizing in unison also permits insecure learners to respond softly, when they are unsure, and strongly, when they are confident. This encourages the most reluctant learners to participate. In addition, the need to respond rapidly induces an extraordinary level of focus and concentration among learners. This intense degree of concentration is experienced by learners as a game. Many observers over the years will attest to this reality. The social dimension of this activity permits learners to experience and enjoy an intense sense of participation (with their peers), in which they are attempting to defeat the teacher who has declared his or her intention to "beat" or "catch" them. Finally, the reluctant learners' expectation that they will be called on to respond to questions on a daily basis will keep them focussed at all times.

Traditional educational practice has generally failed to engage certain types of personalities among learners. Shy, introverted, as well as socially and physically aggressive individuals are, all too often, among the poorest performers in traditional mathematics education classroom strategies. Through the years, however, teachers everywhere have told us (and our data substantiates their claims) that our unison response activities have brought them unprecedented success in engaging the effective participation of the traditionally reluctant learner. This, in turn, has led to a vast improvement of the performance of such students in traditional educational circumstances.

We are convinced, therefore, that these (and many others within our three texts) are pedagogical means whereby the intellects of such individuals can be engaged with respect to their academic objectives, and their capacity for leadership harnessed for the purpose of teaching mathematics to small groups of slow learners. If this is exercised as a deliberate aspect of educational practice, with adequate counseling and training, such individuals will become very able and effective assistants to their teachers. They will acquire a strong sense of self-esteem, self-confidence, self-assurance, and responsibility for the learning of their peers. The youngsters who practice social responsibility in school are likely to be socially responsible adults.

Consider the powerful impact that this phenomenon would make on the prevailing attitudes toward the learning of mathematics. Peer pressure would certainly be transformed from negative to positive, by the very group of individuals who determine what form it should take.

UNDERSTANDING "ONE" THROUGH "TEN"

Objectives: The learners will

(a) name the number of any set of fingers without counting;

(b) show the set of fingers corresponding to any number named from one to nine inclusive; and

(c) instantly name the complement in ten of any number from one to nine inclusive.

Introducing One

Hold up any one of ten fingers, keeping the others clenched, and say to learners, "One finger."

Fold that finger, hold up another and say again, "One finger."

Fold that finger, hold up another and ask, "How many fingers?" (Some learners will answer, "One.")

Keep flicking fingers, holding up one at a time, asking, "How many?" each time until all the learners say, "One," consistently.

Matching Ones

Hold up one finger and ask, "Can you make one like this?"

Hold up many other examples of one finger, each time asking, "Can you make one like this?"

Please note that children must not be urged to match examples of one finger which cause them some discomfort. It will suffice if each child matches the examples which are comfortable.

Showing Different Ones

Tell learners,

"Show me one finger";

"Show me a different one";
"Another one";
"Another";
and so on, until they have shown one finger in many different ways.

Introducing Two

Now hold up two fingers out of ten keeping the others clenched. The two fingers should be at first adjacent; then non-adjacent with both on one hand; and, finally, one on each hand.

When the first set of two fingers is held up, say, "Two fingers."

Hold up a different set of two fingers and ask, "How many fingers?"

Keep flicking different sets of two fingers, each time asking, "How many?" until learners say, "Two," consistently. Frequently surprise them by showing one finger when they are anticipating two.

Matching Twos

Hold up two fingers and ask, "Can you make two like this?"

Hold up many other examples of two fingers, each time asking, "Can you make two like this?"

Children must not be urged to match examples of two fingers which cause them some discomfort. It will suffice if each child matches the examples which are comfortable.

Showing Different Twos

Tell learners,
"Show me two fingers";
"Show me a different two";
"Another two";
"Another";
and so on, until they have facility in showing many different sets of two fingers.

Mixed Practice with Ones and Twos

Having introduced one and two, show fingers and ask questions involving both as follows:
One finger up. "How many?"
Two up. "How many?"
A different two up. "How many?"
A different one up. "How many?"
Two up, "How many?"

One up, "How many?"
Continue similarly, until learners are consistently correct in their responses; **then move on**.

Direct learners as follows:
"Show me one finger."
"Show me a different one."
"Show me two fingers."
"Show me a different one."
"Show me a different two."
Continue similarly until learners have acquired facility; **then move on**.

Introducing Three

Now hold up three fingers out of ten, keeping the others clenched. The three should be at first adjacent; then two of the three adjacent on one hand; then none of the three adjacent on one hand; and, finally, two on one hand, and one on the other.

When the first set of three fingers is held up, say, "Three fingers."

Keep flicking different sets of three fingers, each time asking, "How many?" until learners say, "Three," consistently.

Frequently surprise them by showing one or two fingers when they are anticipating three.

Matching Threes

Hold up three fingers and ask, "Can you make three like this?"

Hold up many other examples of three fingers, each time asking, "Can you make three like this?"

Children must not be urged to match examples of three fingers which cause them some discomfort. It will suffice if each child matches the examples which are comfortable.

Showing Different Threes

Tell learners,
"Show me three fingers";
"Show me a different three";
"Another three";
"Another";
and so on, until they have facility in showing many different sets of three fingers.

Mixed Practice with Ones, Twos, and Threes

Mix up ones, twos, and threes, by flicking, very quickly, different sets of one, two, or three fingers, each time asking, "How many?"

Continue similarly until learners are consistently correct in their answers.

When you hold up a set of fingers, **be sure you do not give children time to count them**. Your objective is to get an instant recognition of the number associated with a set of fingers.

This ability prevents children from developing the burdensome finger counting habit which is a nightmare to most teachers in elementary schools.

Direct learners as follows:
"Show me two fingers";
"Show me three fingers";
"Show me two fingers";
"A different two";
"Show me one finger";
"Show me three fingers";
"A different three";
"Show me one finger";
"A different one";
and so on.

Practice to the level of facility; **then move on**.

Introducing Four

Hold up four fingers out of ten, keeping the others clenched. The four should be at first adjacent on one hand (either one of the "end" fingers down); then non-adjacent (any one of the three middle fingers down) on one hand; then any three on one hand and any one on the other; and, finally, any two on one hand and any two on the other.

Frequently surprise them by showing one, two, or three fingers when they are anticipating four.

Matching Fours

Hold up four fingers and ask, "Can you make four like this?"

Hold up many other examples of four fingers, each time asking, "Can you make four like this?"

Children must not be urged to match examples of four fingers which cause them some discomfort. It will suffice if each child matches the examples which are comfortable.

Showing Different Fours

Have learners demonstrate their ability to show a wide variety of different fours on their fingers.

Mixed Practice with Ones, Twos, Threes, and Fours

Mix up ones, twos, threes, and fours by flicking, very quickly, different sets of one, two, three, or four fingers, each time asking, "How many?"

Be sure you do not give children time to count. Instant recognition of the number of fingers is very important.

Direct learners to show different numbers of fingers from one to four.

Practice to the level of facility; **then move on**.

Introducing Five

Hold up five fingers out of ten, keeping the others clenched. The five should be at first adjacent (all five on one hand); then any four on one hand and any one on the other; and finally, any three on one hand and any two on the other.

Frequently surprise them by showing one, two, three, or four fingers when they are anticipating five.

Matching Fives

Hold up five fingers and ask, "Can you make five like this?"

Hold up many other examples of five fingers, each time asking, "Can you make five like this?"

Children must not be urged to match examples of five fingers which cause them some discomfort. It will suffice if each child matches the examples which are comfortable.

Showing Different Fives

Have learners demonstrate their ability to show a wide variety of fives on their fingers.

Mixed Practice with Ones, Twos, Threes, Fours, and Fives

Mix up ones, twos, threes, fours and fives by flicking, very quickly, different sets of one, two, three, four, and five fingers, each time asking, "How many?".

Be sure you do not give children time to count. Instant recognition of the number of fingers is very important.

Direct learners to show different numbers of fingers from one to five.

Practice to the level of facility; **then move on**.

Introducing Ten and Nine

Learners usually have much more difficulty recognizing six, seven, eight or nine fingers than two, three, four, or five.

Since ten fingers are rather easily recognized, the author advises that you skip from recognition of five fingers to recognition of ten.

Hold up ten fingers and say, "Ten fingers."

Mix up ones, twos, threes, fours, fives, and tens, by flicking different sets of one, two, three, four, five, and ten fingers (there is only one set of ten fingers). Ask, "How many?" each time.

In order to introduce nine, hold up all fingers and ask, "How many?" (Children respond, "Ten")

Now fold just one finger and ask, "Is this still ten?" (Children respond, "No")

Tell learners, "These are nine because one is down."

Now ask, "Why are these nine?" (Children respond, "Because one is down")

Hold up ten fingers again and fold a different one. Ask, "How many?"

Tell learners, "These are nine because one is down."

Now ask, "Why are these nine?" (Children respond, "Because one is down")

Place both hands behind your back and fold one finger.

Quickly show your fingers and ask, "How many?"

When learners promptly answer, "Nine!" ask, "How did you know so fast? Did you have to count or could you just look and tell?" (Children respond, "Look and tell")

Repeat the above many times, each time asking, "How do you know these are nine?" ("Because one is down") The learners will soon recognize nine fingers by the process of looking at "one down" and knowing "nine up."

Note that learners now recognize nine fingers without having to count from one through nine.

As you continue to show nine or ten fingers and ask, "How many?" you should frequently surprise them by showing one, two, three, four, or five fingers when they anticipate ten or nine.

Matching Tens and Nines

Hold up nine fingers and ask, "Can you make nine like this?"

Hold up many other examples of nine fingers, each time asking, "Can you make nine like this?"

Children must not be urged to match examples of nine fingers which cause them some discomfort. It will suffice if each child matches the examples which are comfortable.

Showing Different Nines

Have learners demonstrate their ability to show a wide variety of nines on their fingers.

Mixed Practice with Ones, Twos, Threes, Fours, Fives, Tens, and Nines

Mix up ones, twos, threes, fours, fives, tens, and nines by flicking, very quickly, different sets of one, two, three, four, five, ten, or nine fingers, each time asking, "How many?"

Be sure you do not give children time to count. Instant recognition of the number of fingers is very important.

Direct learners to show different numbers of fingers from one through five, ten, and nine.

Practice to the level of facility; **then move on**.

Introducing Eight

In order to introduce eight, hold up all fingers and ask, "How many?"

Now fold any two and ask, "Are these still ten?" (Children respond, "No") "Are these nine?" ("No")

Tell learners, "These are eight because two are down."

Now ask, "Why are these eight?" (Children respond, "Because two are down")

Hold up ten fingers again and fold two different fingers.

Ask, "How many?"

Tell learners, "These are eight because two are down."

Now ask, "Why are these eight?" (Learners respond, "Because two are down")

Place both hands behind your back and fold two fingers.

Quickly show your fingers and ask, "How many?"

When learners answer, "Eight!" ask, "How did you know so fast? Did you have to count or could you just look and tell?"

Repeat the above many times, each time asking, "How do you know these are eight?" ("Because two are down") The learners will soon recognize eight fingers by the process of looking at "two down" and knowing "eight up."

Note that learners now recognize eight fingers without having to count from one through eight.

As you continue to show eight fingers and ask, "How many?" you should frequently surprise them by showing one, two, three, four, five, ten, or nine fingers when they anticipate eight.

Matching Eights

Hold up eight fingers and ask, "Can you make eight like this?"

Hold up many other examples of eight fingers, each time asking, "Can you make eight like this?"

Children must not be urged to match examples of eight fingers which cause them some discomfort. It will suffice if each child matches the examples which are comfortable.

Showing Different Eights

Have learners demonstrate their ability to show a wide variety of eights on their fingers.

Mixed Practice with Ones, Twos, Threes, Fours, Fives, Tens, Nines, and Eights

Mix up ones, twos, threes, fours, fives, tens, nines, and eights by flicking, very quickly, different sets of one, two, three, four, five, ten, nine, or eight fingers, each time asking, "How many?"

Be sure you do not give children time to count. Instant recognition of the number of fingers is very important.

Direct learners to show different numbers of fingers from one through five, ten, nine, and eight.

Practice to the level of facility; **then move on**.

Introducing Seven

In order to introduce seven, hold up all fingers and ask, "How many?"

Now fold any three and ask:
"Are these ten?" (Children respond, "No")
"Are these nine?" ("No")
"Are these eight?" ("No")

Tell learners, "These are seven because three are down."

Hold up ten again, and fold three different fingers.

Ask, "How many?"

Tell learners, "These are seven because three are down."

Now ask, "Why are these seven?" (Learners respond, "Because three are down")

Place both hands behind your back and fold three fingers.

Quickly show your fingers and ask, "How many?"

When they answer, "Seven!" ask, "How did you know so fast? Did you have to count or could you just look and tell?"

Repeat the above many times, each time asking, "How do you know these are seven?" ("Because three are down") The learners will soon recognize seven fingers by the process of looking at "three down" and knowing "seven up."

Note that learners now recognize seven fingers without having to count from one through seven.

As you continue to show seven fingers and ask, "How many?" you should frequently surprise them by showing one, two, three, four, five, ten, nine, or eight fingers when they anticipate seven.

Matching Sevens

Hold up seven fingers and ask, "Can you make seven like this?"

Hold up many other examples of seven fingers, each time asking, "Can you make seven like this?"

Children must not be urged to match examples of seven fingers which cause them some discomfort. It will suffice if each child matches the examples which are comfortable.

Showing Different Sevens

Have learners demonstrate their ability to show a wide variety of sevens on their fingers.

Mixed Practice with Ones, Twos, Threes, Fours, Fives, Tens, Nines, Eights, and Sevens

Mix up ones, twos, threes, fours, fives, tens, nines, eights, and sevens by flicking, very quickly, different sets of one, two, three, four, five, ten, nine, eight, or seven fingers, each time asking, "How many?"

Be sure you do not give children time to count. Instant recognition of the number of fingers is very important.

Direct learners to show different numbers of fingers from one through five, ten, nine, eight, and seven.

Practice to the level of facility; **then move on**.

Introducing Six

In order to introduce six, hold up all fingers and ask, "How many?"

Now fold any four and ask,
"Are these eight?" (Children respond, "No.")
"Are these seven?" ("No")

Tell learners, "These are six because four are down."

Now ask, "Why are these six?" (Learners respond, "Because four are down.")

Place both hands behind your back and fold four fingers.

Quickly show your fingers and ask, "How many?"

When they answer, "Six!" ask, "How did you know so fast? Did you have to count or could you just look and tell?"

Repeat the above many times, each time asking, "How do you know these are six?" ("Because four are down.") The learners will soon recognize six fingers by the process of looking at "four down" and knowing "six up."

Note that learners now recognize six fingers without having to count from one to six.

As you continue to show six fingers and ask, "How many?" you should frequently surprise them by showing one, two, three, four, five, ten, nine, eight, or seven when they anticipate six.

Matching Sixes

Hold up six fingers and ask, "Can you make six like this?"

Hold up many other examples of six fingers, each time asking, "Can you make six like this?"

Children must not be urged to match examples of six fingers which cause them some discomfort. It will suffice if each child matches the examples which are comfortable.

Showing Different Sixes

Have learners demonstrate their ability to show a wide variety of different sixes on their fingers.

Mixed Practice with Ones, Twos, Threes, Fours, Fives, Tens, Nines, Eights, Sevens, and Sixes

Mix up ones, twos, threes, fours, fives, tens, nines, eights, sevens, and sixes by flicking, very quickly, different sets of one, two, three, four, five, ten, nine, eight, seven, or six fingers, each time asking, "How many?"

Be sure you do not give children time to count. Instant recognition of the number of fingers is very important.

Direct learners to show different numbers of fingers from one through five, ten, nine, eight, seven, and six.

Practice to the level of facility; **then move on.**

The two games described below are designed to establish strong mental linkages between 9 and 1, 8 and 2, 7 and 3, 6 and 4.

Playing with the Complements in Ten

Tell the learners to hold up all ten fingers.

Explain to them that if you say, "Nine!" they must, as quickly as possible, put one finger down. If you say, "Eight!" they must immediately put two down. "Seven!" triggers three down and "Six!" triggers four down.

The game may now proceed as follows:

"Everybody put up ten fingers."
"Ready, eight!" (As children scramble to put the proper number of fingers down, you should rapidly look at many different pairs of hands to check their responses)
"Back to ten."
"Ready, six!" (Rapidly look at many different pairs of hands)
"Back to ten."
"Ready, nine!" (Rapidly check many different pairs of hands)

Continue similarly for 5 minutes.

Practice this activity for 5 minutes each day until children have achieved mastery.

Equivalent Subsets of Fingers

Learners will transform a three (or nine, or eight, or seven, or six, or five, or four, or two, or one) to a different three (nine, eight, seven, six, five, four, two, one) by means of the procedure below.

Have learners hold up three fingers, palms toward their faces.

Tell them to "put down" one of the three fingers and "put up" a new one.

Ask, "How many?" (3)

Again, have them put down one of the three and put up a new one.

Ask, "How many?" (3)

Have them put up a new finger, and put down one of the three. Ask,
"How many?" (3)
"Put down one and put up another. How many?" (3)
"Put up one. How many?" (4)
"One up, one down. How many?" (4)
"One up, one down. How many?" (4)
"One up, one down. How many?" (4)
"One up. How many?" (5)
"One down, one up. How many?" (5)

Continue these exercises until learners know that, "one down, one up," or "one up, one down" does not change the number, but does change the set of fingers.

We now have a means of transforming from one set of nine (or eight, or seven, and so on) to a different nine (or eight, or seven, and so on).

By means of this technique, your learners can respond confidently when you direct them as follows:
"Show me seven fingers."
"A different seven."
"A different seven."

Repeat this many more times.

Have the learners also see that "two up, two down," "three down, three up," and so on, changes only the set (of fingers); but does not change the number (of fingers).

Have the learners practice using "two down, two up," "three up, three down," and so on, as a means of transforming from one set to another while conserving number.

The teacher should ask learners to perform tasks in Facility Exercises #1 (Workbook I). Please note: this activity is **oral**.

Practice to the level of facility; **then move on.**

LEARNING TO COUNT FROM ONE TO TEN

Objective: The learners will count from one to ten: forward and backward.

From the previous activity, learners will have facility in naming the number of any set of fingers held before them. They should also have facility in responding correctly to requests such as: "Show me seven fingers"; "Show me four fingers"; and so on.

Have learners look at their two hands with all fingers folded and palms facing them.

Now have them unfold fingers sequentially, one at a time, starting with the left thumb (once unfolded, a finger stays unfolded).

As the fingers unfold, have learners say the number which they see: "One, two, three, four, five, six, seven, eight, nine, ten." When they get to ten, they will have all of their fingers extended; palms facing them.

Now have learners fold the right thumb and say, "Nine," in reference to the fingers still extended.

Then have them fold the next finger from the right (that is, the right index finger), so there are now two fingers folded.

Have them say, "Eight," in reference to the fingers which are still extended.

Have them continue to fold fingers from the right so that, in effect, the learners are counting backward.

Have learners play at this activity until they have facility. Eventually, they will be ready to recite the counting sequence forward and backward, without the use of fingers.

It is important that learners acquire **mental facility** in saying the counting sequence forward and backward.

The teacher can now give learners much practice at answering questions such as:

"How many apples are in this box?"
"How many books are on this table?"

At this point, the quantities should be no greater than ten.

Have learners answer the questions below without use of fingers. Be sure they practice on these until facility is achieved; **then move on.**

The teacher should ask individual learners to perform each task in Facility Exercises #2 (Workbook I). Please note: this activity is **oral**.

If the learners have not yet learned the names of the symbols 1, 2, 3, 4, 5, 6, 7, 8, 9, and 10, you may proceed as follows below.

Write the following on the board:

1, 2, 3, 4, 5, 6, 7, 8, 9, 10

Point to the "1" and say, "This says one."

Point to it again and ask, "What does this say?"

Have the learners say, "One," every time you touch 1 on the board (touch it three or four times).

Now point to the "2" and say, "This says two."

Point to it again and ask, "What does this say?"

Have the learners say, "Two," every time you touch 2 on the board (touch it 2 or 3 times).

Now rapidly alternate between touching 1 and 2 (on a few occasions, surprise them by touching the same thing twice), while children respond appropriately in unison.

When they have mastered this (in less than two minutes), point to the "3" and say, "This says three."

Point to it again and ask, "What does this say?"

Now rapidly and randomly touch 1, 2 or 3 (do not touch them in the same order over and over again), while children respond appropriately in unison.

When they have mastered this (you are now less than four minutes into your lesson), proceed similarly up to 4, then 5, and so on, up to 10.

Children will have learned the names of these numerals in three lessons, of less than fifteen minutes each.

Now that the learners know the names of the digits above, teach them how to write the symbols.

Practice to the level of facility; **then move on.**

COUNTING BY TWOS, THREES, FOURS

Objectives: The learners will use fingers for

(a) counting by twos, starting from zero, or one, up to ten, or nine, respectively; forward and backward.

(b) counting by threes, starting from zero, one, or two, up to nine, ten, or eight, respectively; forward and backward.

(c) counting by fours, starting from zero, one, two, or three, up to eight, nine, ten, or seven, respectively; forward and backward.

Before proceeding with the activity below, tell learners the following: "I am going to do something with you. As we work, I want you to concentrate. Listen very carefully to your own words as you say them."

With palms of their hands facing them, have learners hold up the two fingers on the left of their left hands (all other fingers folded).

Ask, "How many?"

Have them hold up the next two from the left (four fingers are now unfolded).

Again ask, "How many?"

Have them hold up the next two (six fingers now unfolded).

Ask, "How many?"

Continue similarly until they unfold ten fingers.

Now ask each learner to repeat the words, "Two, four, six, eight, ten."

Practice until learners have facility in counting aloud by twos to ten; and in using fingers to count as follows: "Two plus two, four; plus two, six; plus two, eight; plus two, ten."

With all their fingers extended, and palms facing them, ask learners, "How many?"

Have them fold the two fingers on the right of their right hands (all other fingers extended).

Ask, "How many?"

Have them fold the next two from the right.

Ask, "How many?"

Continue similarly until they fold all ten fingers.

Now ask each learner to repeat the words, "Ten, eight, six, four, two."

Practice until learners have facility in counting aloud, going backward, by twos from ten, and in using fingers to count (backward) as follows: "Ten take away two, eight; take away two, six; take away two, four; take away two, two."

Learners can use fingers for counting by twos, starting from one, by means of the activity described below.

Have them fold fingers on both hands with palms facing them.

Since they have to start from one, have them unfold the left thumb.

Ask, "How many?" They now have to count by twos. So have them raise the two fingers next to the left thumb.

Ask, "How many?"

Have them raise the next two fingers.

Ask, "How many?"

Continue similarly until they get to nine.

Now ask each learner to repeat the words, "One, three, five, seven, nine."

Practice until learners have facility in counting aloud by twos to nine (starting from one), and in using fingers to count as follows: "One plus two, three; plus two, five; plus two, seven; plus two, nine."

With nine fingers extended, ask learners, "How many?"

Have them fold two. Ask, "How many?"

Have them fold two more.

Ask, "How many?"

Continue similarly until they get to one.

Now ask each learner to repeat the words, "Nine, seven, five, three, one."

Practice until learners have facility in counting aloud, going backward, by twos from nine, and in using fingers to count (backward) as follows: "Nine take away two, seven; take away two, five; take away two, three; take away two, one."

Learners can use fingers for counting by threes, starting from zero, by means of the activity described below.

With palms of their hands facing them, have learners hold up the three fingers on the left of the left hand (all other fingers folded).

Ask, "How many?"

Have them hold up the next three from the left.

Again ask, "How many?"

Have them hold up the next three. "How many?"

Now ask each learner to repeat the words, "Three, six, nine."

Practice until learners have facility in counting aloud by threes to nine, and in using fingers to count as follows: "Three plus three, six; plus three, nine."

When they have acquired facility in counting forward by threes to nine, you may have learners practice counting backward from nine by threes, and in using fingers to count (backward) as follows: "Nine take away three, six; take away three, three."

Learners can use fingers for counting by threes, starting from one, by means of the activity described below.

Have them fold fingers on both hands with palms facing them.

Since they have to start from one, have them unfold the left thumb.

Ask, "How many?"

They now have to count by threes; so have them raise the three fingers next to the left thumb.

Ask, "How many?"

Have them raise the next three fingers.

Ask, "How many?"

Finally, have them raise the next three. "How many?"

Now ask each learner to repeat the words, "One, four, seven, ten."

Practice until learners have facility in counting aloud by threes, from one to ten, and in using fingers to count as follows: "One plus three, four; plus three, seven; plus three, ten."

When they have acquired finger facility counting by threes, starting from one, you may have learners practice counting backward from ten by three, and in using fingers to count (backward) as follows: "Ten take away three, seven; take away three, four; take away three, one."

Learners can use fingers for counting by threes, starting from two, by means of the activity described below.

Have them fold fingers on both hands with palms facing them.

Since they have to start from two, have them unfold the two fingers on the left of their left hands.

Ask, "How many?"

They now have to count by threes; so have them raise the next three fingers from the left.

Ask, "How many?"

Have them raise the next three fingers.

Ask, "How many?"

Now ask learners to repeat the words, "Two, five, eight."

Practice until learners have facility in counting aloud by threes from two to eight, and in using fingers to count as follows: "Two plus three, five; plus three, eight."

When they have acquired finger facility counting by threes, starting from two, you may have learners practice counting backward from eight by threes, and in using fingers to count (backward) as follows: "Eight take away three, five; take away three, two."

You can similarly have learners practice toward facility in counting aloud by

1. fours to eight, using fingers: "Four plus four, eight."
2. fours from eight, using fingers: "Eight take away four, four."
3. fours, starting from one, to nine, using fingers: "One plus four, five; plus four, nine."
4. fours from nine, using fingers: "Nine take away four, five; take away four, one."
5. fours, starting from two, to ten, using fingers: "Two plus four, six; plus four, ten."
6. fours from ten, using fingers: "Ten take away four, six; take away four, two."
7. fours, starting from three, to seven, using fingers: "Three plus four, seven."
8. fours from seven, using fingers: "Seven take away four, three."

You can always return to the pursuit of this counting as a purely mental activity from time to time, at short intervals, as warm-up exercises, for example.

Have learners practice the activities in Facility Exercises #3 (Workbook I) to the level of facility; **then move on.** Please note: this activity is oral.

MORE, LESS, EQUAL

Objective: Given two whole numbers chosen from among the numbers one to ten, the learners will name the larger or the smaller.

Ask each of two learners to hold up four fingers.

Now have one learner match four fingers in a one-to-one correspondence with the four fingers of another learner, by actually touching fingers one-to-one.

Tell learners that since they match one-to-one, the two numbers of fingers are equal.

Ask, "Can three fingers match five fingers in a one-to-one correspondence?"

Have each learner check the response (whether correct or not) by attempting to match three extended fingers with a partner's five, one-to-one.

Ask,
"Which is more; three or five?"
"Which is less; three or five?"

Have learners see that five is more than three since, after the attempted matching, there are two "unmatched" fingers on the hand that shows five.

Be sure learners understand that if five is more than three, it follows that three is less than five.

Ask, "Can six fingers match six fingers in a one-to-one correspondence?"

Have each learner check the response to this question with a partner in the same manner as above.

Ask, "Are the two numbers of fingers equal?"

Repeat this exercise often with equal and unequal numbers until learners arrive at the point where they can tell (mentally) which, of any two whole numbers (from one to ten), is greater or less.

Having learned to count, the learners will be able to rely on the sequence of the sounds as a means of confirming which of two numbers, from one to ten, is greater or less. For example, four is less than seven, since four precedes seven when we count from one to ten.

Have learners answer the questions, without the use of fingers.

Be sure they practice on these questions until facility is achieved; **then move on.**

Ask individual learners the questions in Facility Exercises #4 (Workbook I). Please note: this activity is **oral**.

ADDITION FACTS
(on the fingers)

Objective: The learners will use fingers to add two whole numbers with sum less than, or equal to, ten. **This will be done without counting.**

Instruct learners as follows:
"Hold up five fingers."
"Hold up three more."
"How many fingers altogether?"
Since the learners have already learned to name the number of any set of fingers instantly (without counting), they will respond immediately with "Eight," after showing five fingers, and then three more. **This is appropriate so long as the response comes immediately, and the learners are not counting in order to arrive at the answer.**

Keep repeating this activity with different pairs of numbers, until learners acquire facility in the use of fingers for knowing the basic addition facts.

Modify your instructions to the learners.

Explain to them that when you say, "Show me a 'five-three'," they must **immediately** show five fingers and three more; then, when you ask, "How many?" they must **immediately** give the answer.

Please note that "five-three" is read "fivethree."

Here is another example:
"Show me a 'seven-two'."
"How many?"

Have learners practice this activity to the level of facility; **then move on.**

Please note that the symbolic representation of these questions, such as "3+4=_____," should only be shown to learners after they have facility with the verbal questions.

Remember that you learned to speak before you learned to read!

The learners can now be told that both "3+4" and its vertical representation mean, "Three and four more." Consequently, the sight of the symbols 3+4 must trigger the appropriate response on students' fingers, which immediately yields the answer.

Vertical and horizontal addition examples can now be assigned from Facility Exercises #5 (Workbook I).

Have learners practice these exercises to the level of facility (with fingers - **no counting**); **then move on.**

There are two phases, in our methodology, toward learners' instant recall of the lower addition and subtraction facts (no finger activity necessary):

1. the prescribed use of **Professor B Math Charts (Charts #1, #2 and #3)**; and
2. the intensive involvement with "long additions" and "long subtractions" (numbers involved range from tens of thousands to hundreds of millions) without regrouping or exchanging, during which time, learners' instant and accurate recall of the facts continues to be strengthened.

These phases will be described within this text.

LINKING ADDITION AND SUBTRACTION

Objective: Given an addition fact, sum less than or equal to ten, the learners will use fingers for finding the answers to the related subtraction facts. **This will be done without counting.**

Direct learners as follows:

"Hold up four fingers."
"Hold up two more."
"How many altogether?"
"Now fold four fingers. How many are left?"
"So how many are six 'take away' four?"
"Unfold the four fingers, so that six fingers are again shown."
"Now fold two fingers. How many are left?"
"How many are six take away two?"

"Hold up five fingers."
"Hold up three more."
"How many altogether?"
"Now fold five fingers. How many are left?"
"How many are eight take away five?"
"Unfold the five fingers, so that eight fingers are again shown."
"Now fold three fingers. How many are left?"
"How many are eight take away three?"

"Hold up eight fingers and fold two."
"How many are eight take away two?"
"So how many are six 'put back' two?"
"Hold up eight fingers and fold six."
"How many are eight take away six?"
"So how many are two put back six?"

After much practice in the above activity (with different sets of numbers), introduce the word "plus", by telling the learners that "three plus four" means the same as three and four more.

Have learners answer sets of questions such as those below. Allow use of fingers **(but no counting).**

"How many are three plus four?"
"How many are seven take away three?"
"How many are seven take away four?"

"How many are two plus five?"
"How many are seven take away two?"
"How many are seven take away five?"

Tell learners that both "7–2" and its vertical representation are read as, "Seven take away two."

Have learners practice the examples of Facility Exercises #6 (Workbook I) to the level of facility; **then move on.**

Each set of examples in these exercises shows relationships between addition facts and related subtraction facts.

SUBTRACTION FACTS
(on the fingers)

Objective: The learners will subtract one whole number from a larger whole number (larger number less than or equal to ten) with the use of fingers. **This will be done without counting.**

Ask many subtraction questions in the following way:
"Hold up seven fingers."
"Now fold two fingers."
"How many are seven take away two?"

"Hold up four fingers."
"Now fold three fingers."
"How many are four take away three?"

Continue as above until learners have facility with the appropriate performance on their fingers.

The subtraction questions can now be asked as follows:
"Five take away three. What's the answer?"
"Eight take away five. What's the answer?"

Continue with more of these questions.

Very soon, after explaining that both "minus" and "subtract" mean "take away," you can begin to ask many questions such as (allow learners to use fingers in the prescribed way if they wish):
"Seven minus four equals what?"
"Nine minus six equals what?"
"From eight, take two. What's left?"
"From six, subtract one. What's the answer?"
"Subtract three from ten. What's the answer?"

Continue with more of these questions.

Many subtraction questions should be asked in the various forms.

The symbolic representation of these questions, such as "8–3" for "eight minus three," should only be used after learners have facility with the verbal questions.

Finger facility for answering the subtraction questions is sufficient at this point; although learners' mental mastery of these facts will be strongly accelerated when you use the **Professor B charts** and assign them long subtractions (no exchanging). If fingers are not needed, so much the better.

Have learners use addition for checking their own answers.

In this way, they can rely on themselves for knowing the correctness of their subtractions.

For example, ask, "Six minus two?"

If learners answer, "Three," have them check as follows: "Three plus two equal five; so my answer is wrong since I did not get back six."

If learners answer, "Four," they should check by saying, "Four plus two equal six; so my answer is correct since I got back six."

It will be very helpful if, each time a subtraction is checked, the learner recites as shown above.

The examples and the checking would look like this in writing:

Example	**Learner's Work**	**Check**
6 – 2=___	6 – 2 = _4_	4 + 2 = _6_

It could also look like this:

Example	**Learner's Work**	**Check**
$\begin{array}{r} 6 \\ \underline{-2} \end{array}$	$\begin{array}{r} 6 \\ \underline{-2} \\ 4 \end{array}$	$\begin{array}{r} 2 \\ \underline{+4} \\ 6 \end{array}$

Have learners practice answering and checking the examples of Facility Exercises #7 (Workbook I) to the level of "finger facility"; **then move on.**

ADDING AND SUBTRACTING WITH ZERO

Objective: The learners will do additions and subtractions involving zero (larger number less than or equal to ten). This includes examples in which the answer is zero.

So far in this development, the only appearance of the digit zero has been in the numeral 10.

At this point, we will use the digit zero to represent "no objects."

From their previous experiences, the learners know that 5+2, for example, represents combining a set of five objects with a set of two objects (five and two more), which creates a set of 5+2 objects.

Have learners understand that 5+0, for example, represents combining five objects with no objects.

Ask,

"If we combine five objects with no objects, how many do we have?"
"So the answer to 5+0 is 5."

"What does 7+0 represent?"
"So what is the answer to 7+0?"

"What does 0+3 represent?"
"So what is the answer to 0+3?"

"What is the answer to 6+0? 0+8? 8+0? 0+1? 2+0? 0+0? 10+0? 0+7? 0+4? 9+0? 0+3? 3+0? 0+6? 4+0? 0+10? 0+5?"

It is satisfactory, at this point, if learners (as in previous experiences) say that 7–4 means take away four objects from seven objects.

Ask learners the following questions:

"What does 6–2 mean to you? 9–5? 8–1? 2–1? 5–4? 10–6? 6–3? 7–2? 4–1? 8–4? 3–2? 7–7? 5–5? 9–9? 10–10? 1–1? 4–4?"

"What does 7–0 mean to you?"
"So if we take away zero objects from seven objects, how many are left?"
"So what is the answer to 8–0? 3–0? 10–0? 1–0? 9–0? 4–0? 6–0? 5–0? 2–0?"

"What does 8–8 mean to you?"
"So if we take away eight objects from eight objects, how many are left?" (No objects are left)

"Since the digit zero represents no objects, it follows that the answer to 8–8 is zero."
"What is the answer to 2–2? 9–9? 4–4? 1–1? 10–10? 3–3? 5–5? 7–7? 6–6? 0–0?"

In each example of Facility Exercises #7, be sure to have learners interpret the symbolism before answering.

For example, 8–0 says, "Take away no objects from 8 objects."

Have learners practice the examples of Facility Exercises #8 (Workbook I) to the level of facility; **then move on.**

SUMS AND DIFFERENCES INVOLVING MORE THAN TWO NUMBERS

Objectives: The learners will

(a) find the value of an expression which is a sum of more than two numbers (the value is less than or equal to ten).
(b) find the value of an expression which is a difference that involves more than two numbers (the value is less than or equal to ten).
(c) find the value of an expression which combines sums and differences of more than two numbers.
(d) tell which of two expressions represents a larger number.

Write on the board:

1+2+4+2   9–2–1–3–1   3+4–2–3+1+5–4

Elicit the value of 1+2+4+2 as follows:
Tell learners,

"With palms toward your face, fold all fingers."
"Raise the left thumb." (1)
"Keep the left thumb up. Now since you see a plus sign, raise the next two fingers." (1+2)
"How much is that?"
"Add or raise four more fingers, since you see another plus sign." (1+2+4)
"How much is that?"
"Add two more, since you see one more plus sign." (1+2+4+2)
"How much is that?"

So 1+2+4+2=9.

Elicit the value of 9–2–1–3–1 as follows:
Tell learners,

"With palms toward your face, fold all fingers."
"Since the problem starts off with nine, raise nine fingers." (9)
"Now, since you see a minus sign, fold two fingers." (9–2)
"How much is that ?" (7)
"Fold one more, since you see another minus sign." (9–2–1)

"How much is that?"
"Fold three more. Why?" (9–2–1–3)
"How much is that?"
"Fold one more. Why?" (9–2–1–3–1)
"How many fingers are left?" (2)
So 9–2–1–3–1=2.

Elicit the value of 3+4–2–3+1+5–4 as follows:
Tell learners,
"With palms toward your face, fold all fingers."
"Since the problem starts off with three, raise three fingers." (3)
"Now, since you see a plus sign, raise four fingers." (3+4)
"How much is that?" (7)
"Fold two since you see a minus sign." (3+4–2)
"How much is that?" (5)
"Fold three since you see a minus sign." (3+4–2–3)
"How much is that?" (2)
Continue similarly to raise or fold fingers, as the signs dictate.
Tell learners that they must be very careful to obey the signs.
Eventually they conclude that:

3+4–2–3+1+5–4=4

Elicit answers to the following examples:

6–3+2+4–1   10–6–2+3+3–4   5+3–2+1–4+3

Write on the board:

7+3   8–4–2+3+1–4

Ask, "Which is larger: 7+3 or 8–4–2+3+1–4?"

Elicit from learners that 7+3 represents the larger number.

Have learners practice the examples of Facility Exercises #9 (Workbook I) to the level of facility; **then move on.**

MASTERING THE LOWER ADDITION AND SUBTRACTION FACTS: THE "TEN-CHART" GAME

Objectives: The learners will

1. respond, instantly and accurately, with the complement in ten, of any number chosen from one through nine;
2. respond, instantly and accurately, to symbolic representations of subtraction facts, in which the larger number is ten; and
3. respond, instantly and accurately, to symbolic representations of addition facts, for which the sum is ten.

Carefully follow the unison response activity instructions (see page one), as you lead your learners through the techniques of this section once per day, for two or three days.

Place the chart below on the blackboard.

(10)	
9	1
8	2
7	3
6	4
5	5

By holding up ten fingers (palms facing the learners) and wiggling the "little finger" (at the end), be sure learners agree that 9 and 1 are ten.

Proceed similarly for 8 and 2, 7 and 3, 6 and 4, 5 and 5.

Now explain to learners that they must respond aloud and in unison with "One," when you say, "Nine," or "Nine," when you say, "One"; with "Eight," when you say, "Two," or "Two," when you say, "Eight"; with "Seven," when you say, "Three," or "Three," when you say, "Seven"; with "Four," when you say, "Six," or "Six," when you say, "Four"; and with "Five," when you say, "Five."

This is to be done in a "rapid-fire" manner, just as fast as children can go, while keeping their voices in unison.

Be absolutely certain that ALL EYES are "glued" to the chart.

When the sound of their voices in unison indicates they are confident and consistently correct in their responses (in 3 to 4 minutes), it is time to stop and challenge the slowest learners (in particular) to give four or five responses by themselves.

It is very important that you do not permit any other individual to provide a response for the learner you called upon.

At this point, erase the 1 and the 8.

Challenge the learners as follows: "Now let's see if you can remember the numbers I have erased."

Alternatively, tap the empty spaces for less than one minute (try to catch them), as learners respond (in unison) with the numbers which were erased.

Now erase the 3, and challenge them again: "I think I'll beat you this time."

Tap on the three empty spaces (keep changing the sequence as you try to catch them), for less than one minute as learners respond in unison.

Now erase the 6, and challenge them again: "You beat me last time, but I think I will win this time."

Tap on the four empty spaces (keep changing the sequence) for less than one minute, (you will be able to make at least 30 taps in one minute) as they respond in unison.

At this point, you might call on the slowest learners (in particular) to respond, individually, to three or four taps.

Proceed similarly to tap randomly on the five empty spaces (as learners respond in unison), after the 5 (on the right) has been erased.

At this point, return to the original game in which you say a number (chosen from one through nine) and the learners respond in unison with its complement in ten.

For example, if you say, "Three" they say, "Seven."

Continue this activity for 3 to 4 minutes before checking for individual responses from the slowest learners in particular.

You must now resume the erasing of numbers.

Erase the 9, challenge the learners, and begin to tap randomly on the six empty spaces (as learners respond in unison) for one minute.

Erase the 2, challenge the learners, and tap randomly on the seven empty spaces (as learners respond in unison) for one minute.

Continue similarly until the 7, the 4 and the 5 have been erased.

There are now no numbers on the chart (except for the 10).

Once again, return to the original game in which you say a number (chosen from one through nine) and the learners respond in unison with its complement in ten.

Continue this activity for 3 to 4 minutes before checking for individual responses from the slowest learners in particular.

The learners can now respond instantly with the complement in ten, whenever you say any of the numbers, from one through nine.

Repeat this entire 10-Chart game, starting from scratch, for one or two more lessons.

After these two or three days, learners must never see numbers in the 10-Chart again.

Learners will now have mastered the 10-Chart to the extent that they are able to respond, instantly and accurately, with the complement in ten of any number from one through nine.

This mastery, once attained, will be sustained by means of the **daily** activities described below (remember that learners must never see numbers in the ten-chart again).

Conduct those activities (below) with your learners for two consecutive lessons.

Activity #1: First recitation exercise

Have each learner recite as follows: "Ten nine, one; ten eight, two; ten seven, three; ten six, four; ten five, five; ten five, five; ten four, six; ten three, seven; ten two, eight; ten one, nine."

Be sure learners practice this **daily** until it has been mastered by all participants.

Activity #2: Second recitation exercise

Have each learner recite as follows: "Nine one, ten; eight two, ten; seven three, ten; six four, ten; five five, ten; five five, ten; four six, ten; three seven, ten; two eight, ten; one nine, ten."

Be sure learners practice this **daily,** until it has been mastered by all participants.

Activity #3: Auditory stimulus, auditory response

Have learners respond rapidly to questions such as, "Ten four?" (they respond, "Six"); "Ten eight?" (they respond, "Two"); "Ten five?" (they respond, "Five"); and so on.

Engage them in this activity for four minutes per day for the two consecutive lessons.

Activity #4: Visual stimulus, auditory response

Have learners respond rapidly and accurately when you tap 10–1, 10–2, 10–3, 10–4, through 10–9 (vary the sequence through which you tap these facts) on the **Professor B Math Chart #2** (the Lower Subtraction Facts).

These appear on the chart in various positions within an array consisting of all the lower subtraction facts.

Engage them in this activity for four minutes per day for the two consecutive lessons.

Activity #5: Visual stimulus, auditory response

Have learners respond rapidly and accurately when you tap 9+1, 8+2, 7+3, 6+4, 5+5, 4+6, 3+7, 2+8, and 1+9 (vary the sequence through which you tap these facts) on the **Professor B Math Chart #3** (the Lower Addition Facts).

These appear on the chart in various positions within an array consisting of all the lower addition facts.

Engage them in this activity for three minutes per day for the two consecutive lessons.

Activity #6: Class work and homework exercises

Immediately following the second lesson, covering Activities #1 through #5, you must give learners class work and, afterward, assign homework involving a random mix of addition and subtraction (some horizontal, some vertical), using the facts in Activities #4 and #5.

Continue to give this type of class work and homework for the next four days.

These exercises are found in Workbook I.

Have learners practice the examples of Facility Exercises #10 through #17 (Workbook I) to the level of facility; **then move on**.

MASTERING THE LOWER ADDITION AND SUBTRACTION FACTS: THE "NINE-CHART" GAME

Objectives: The learners will

1. respond, instantly and accurately, with the complement in nine, of any number chosen from one through eight;
2. respond, instantly and accurately, to symbolic representations of subtraction facts, in which the larger number is nine; and
3. respond, instantly and accurately, to symbolic representations of addition facts, for which the sum is nine.

For the next two or three lessons after you have practiced Activities #1 through #5 for the 10-Chart, first convince the learners, by means of fingers and manipulative materials, that 8 and 1, 7 and 2, 6 and 3, 5 and 4 all equal 9; then carefully follow the unison response activity instructions (see page one), as you lead your learners through the techniques of this section once per day, for two or three days.

For these two or three days, please **remember to practice Activities #1 through #6 for the 10-Chart**, as well as the two recitation exercises for the 10-Chart, before working with the 9-Chart as described below.

Now place the following on the board:

(9)	
8	1
7	2
6	3
5	4

Before you begin to work on the 9-Chart, it is **very important** that you "spell out" exactly the way in which you expect to catch them in the 9-Chart game. Tell them you think they are going to forget they are working on nine, and give you the responses for ten.

Take the time to "rub it in"; you just can't wait to catch them thinking about ten, instead of nine. If you do this well, you will be very surprised at the smooth transition from the 10-Chart to the 9-Chart.

Now proceed similarly as you did with the 10-Chart for two or three consecutive lessons (see below).

Step 1

With all learners looking intently on the 9-Chart (all the numbers in it), say any one of the numbers from one through eight.

Learners must quickly respond with its complement in nine.

Continue with this rapid-response activity for 3 to 4 minutes.

Step 2

Gradually erase 1, 7, 3, and 5, while tapping the empty spaces, and having learners rapidly respond by saying the missing numbers.

This should take about 3 minutes.

Step 3

With half of the numbers missing, return to the original game (Step 1) in which you say any one of the numbers from one through eight, and learners respond accordingly.

Continue this for about 3 minutes.

Step 4

Resume the erasing (one at a time) and tapping of the empty spaces; while learners rapidly respond with the missing numbers.

Continue this until all numbers (except the 9) have been erased. This should take about 3 minutes.

Step 5

With all the numbers missing, return, once more, to the original game (Step 1) in which you say any one of the numbers from one through eight, and learners respond accordingly.

Continue this for about 3 minutes.

Repeat this entire 9-Chart game, starting from scratch, for one or two more lessons.

Remember to begin these lessons with a review of Activities #1 through #6 for the 10-Chart.

After these two or three lessons, learners must never see numbers in the 9-Chart again.

Learners will now have mastered the 9-Chart to the extent that they are able to instantly and accurately respond with the complement in nine of any number from one through eight.

This mastery, once attained, will be sustained by means of the activities described below (remember that learners must never see numbers in the 9- or 10-Charts again).

Conduct those activities with your learners for two consecutive lessons.

Please remember! Those activities (below) must be preceded by a review of Activities #1 through #6 for the 10-Chart.

Activity #1: First recitation exercise

Have each learner recite as follows: "Nine eight, one; nine seven, two; nine six, three; nine five, four; nine four, five; nine three, six; nine two, seven; nine one, eight."

Be sure learners practice this **daily,** until it has been mastered by all participants.

Activity #2: Second recitation exercise

Have each learner recite as follows: "Eight one, nine; seven two, nine; six three, nine; five four, nine; four five, nine; three six, nine; two seven, nine; one eight, nine."

Be sure learners practice this **daily,** until it has been mastered by all participants.

Activity #3: Auditory stimulus, auditory response

Have learners respond rapidly to questions such as, "Nine five?" (they respond, "Four"); "Nine two?" (they respond, "Seven"); "Nine six?" (they respond, "Three"); and so on.

Engage them in this activity for four minutes per day for the two consecutive lessons.

Activity #4: Visual stimulus, auditory response

Have learners respond, rapidly and accurately, when you tap 9–1, 9–2, 9–3, through 9–8 (vary the sequence through which you tap these facts) on the **Professor B Math Chart #2** (the Lower Subtraction Facts).

These appear on the chart in various positions within an array consisting of all the lower subtraction facts.

Engage them in this activity for four minutes per day for the two consecutive lessons.

Activity #5: Visual stimulus, auditory response

Have learners respond, rapidly and accurately, when you tap 8+1, 7+2, 6+3, 5+4, 4+5, 3+6, 2+7, and 1+8 (vary the sequence through which you tap these facts) on the **Professor B Math Chart #3** (the Lower Addition Facts).

These appear on the chart in various positions, within an array consisting of all the lower addition facts.

Engage them in this activity for three minutes per day for the two consecutive lessons.

Activity #6: Class work and homework exercises

Immediately following the second lesson covering Activities #1 through #5, you must give learners class work and, afterward, assign homework involving a random mix of addition and subtraction (some horizontal, some vertical) using the facts in Activities #4 and #5 for both the 10- and 9-Charts.

Continue to give this type of class work and homework for the next six days.

These exercises are found in Workbook I.

Have learners practice the examples of Facility Exercises #18 through #25 (Workbook I) to the level of facility; **then move on**.

Activities #1 through #5 above must be done for two lessons only.

Following these two lessons, they (the activities) must be replaced by the mixed practice activities described in the next section.

MIXED PRACTICE WITH THE 10- AND 9-CHARTS

Objectives: The learners will

1. respond, instantly and accurately, with the complement in ten or nine, of any number chosen from one through nine, or one through eight, respectively, when given mixed practice involving both;
2. respond, instantly and accurately, to symbolic representations of subtraction facts, in which the larger number is either ten or nine, when given mixed practice involving both; and
3. respond, instantly and accurately, to symbolic representations of addition facts, for which the sum is ten or nine, when given mixed practice involving both.

This mixed practice must be conducted at the beginning of every lesson for the next six days.

On these days, please remember to practice the two recitation exercises for both the 10- and the 9-Charts.

Activity #1: Auditory stimulus, auditory response

Have learners respond rapidly and accurately to questions such as, "Ten three?", "Nine five?", "Ten one?", "Nine two?", "Ten five?", "Nine six?", and so on.

Try to catch them.

Engage them in this activity for four minutes per day for the first two of the six consecutive lessons.

Reduce the amount of time over the next four days.

Activity #2: Visual stimulus, auditory response

Have learners respond rapidly and accurately when you tap such sequences of facts as 10–6, 9–7, 10–2, 9–3, 9–7, 10–9, 10–4, and 9–4 (vary the sequence through which you tap these facts) on the **Professor B Math Chart #2** (the Lower Subtraction Facts).

Try to catch them.

Engage them in this activity for four minutes per day for the first two of the six consecutive lessons.

Reduce the amount of time over the next four days.

Activity #3: Visual stimulus, auditory response

Have learners respond rapidly and accurately when you tap such sequences of facts as 5+5, 6+3, 8+2, 9+1, 7+2, 4+6, 5+4, and 2+7 (vary the sequence through which you tap these facts) on the **Professor B Math Chart #3** (the Lower Addition Facts).

Try to catch them.

Engage them in this activity for four minutes per day for the first two of the six consecutive lessons.

Reduce the amount of time over the next four days.

Activity #4: Class work and homework exercises

Continue (for the next six lessons) to assign mixed practice class work and homework, involving addition and subtraction (some horizontal, some vertical), using the facts from Activity #2 and #3 in this section.

MASTERING THE LOWER ADDITION AND SUBTRACTION FACTS: THE "EIGHT-CHART" GAME

Objectives: The learners will

1. respond, instantly and accurately, with the complement in eight, of any number chosen from one through seven;
2. respond, instantly and accurately, to symbolic representations of subtraction facts, in which the larger number is eight; and,
3. respond, instantly and accurately, to symbolic representations of addition facts, for which the sum is eight.

For the next two or three lessons after you have practiced Activities #1 through #4 (mixed practice with the 10- and 9-Charts), first convince the learners, by means of fingers and manipulative materials, that 7 and 1, 6 and 2, 5 and 3, 4 and 4 all equal 8; then carefully follow the unison response activity instructions (see page one), as you lead your learners through the techniques of this section once per day, for two or three days.

For these two or three days, please **remember to practice Activities #1 through #4 for the 10- and 9-Charts** (mixed practice), as well as the two recitation exercises for each of them, before working with the 8-Chart as described below.

Now place the following on the board:

⑧	
7	1
6	2
5	3
4	4

Before you begin to work on the 8-Chart, it is **very important** that you "spell out" exactly the way in which you expect to catch them in the 8-Chart game: tell them they will forget they are working on eight and give you the responses for ten or nine.

Take the time to "rub it in"; you just can't wait to catch them thinking about ten or nine instead of eight.

If you do this well, you will be very surprised at the smooth transition from the 9-Chart to the 8-Chart.

Now proceed similarly as you did with the 9-Chart for two or three consecutive lessons (see below).

Step 1

With all learners looking intently on the 8-Chart (all the numbers in it), say any one of the numbers from one through seven.

Learners must quickly respond with its complement in eight.

Continue with this rapid-response activity for 3 to 4 minutes.

Step 2

Gradually erase 1, 6, 3, and 4, while tapping the empty spaces, and having learners rapidly respond by saying the missing numbers.

This should take about 3 minutes.

Step 3

With half of the numbers missing, return to the original game (Step 1) in which you say any one of the numbers, from one through seven, and learners respond accordingly.

Continue this for about 3 minutes.

Step 4

Resume the erasing (one at a time) and tapping of the empty spaces, while learners rapidly respond with the missing numbers.

Continue this until all numbers (except the 8) have been erased.

This should take about 3 minutes.

Step 5

With all the numbers missing, return, once more, to the original game (Step 1) in which you say any one of the numbers, from one through seven, and learners respond accordingly.

Continue this for about 3 minutes.

Repeat this entire 8-Chart game, starting from scratch, for one or two more lessons.

Remember to begin these lessons with a review of Activities #1 through #4 for the 10- and 9-Charts (mixed practice), as well as the two recitation exercises for each of them.

After these two or three lessons, learners must never see numbers in the 8-Chart again.

Learners will now have mastered the 8-Chart to the extent that they are able to instantly and accurately respond, with the complement in eight, of any number from one through seven.

This mastery, once attained, will be sustained by means of the activities described below (remember that learners must never see numbers in the 8-, 9-, or 10-Charts again).

Conduct those activities with your learners for two consecutive lessons.

Please remember! Those activities (below) must be preceded by a review of Activities #1 through #4 for the 10- and 9-Charts, as well as the two recitation exercises for each of them.

Activity #1: First recitation exercise

Have each learner recite as follows: "Eight seven, one; eight six, two; eight five, three; eight four, four; eight four, four; eight three, five; eight two, six; eight one, seven."

Be sure learners practice this **daily,** until it has been mastered by all participants.

Activity #2: Second recitation exercise

Have each learner recite as follows: "Seven one, eight; six two, eight; five three, eight; four four, eight; four four, eight; three five, eight; two six, eight; one seven, eight."

Be sure learners practice this **daily**, until it has been mastered by all participants.

Activity #3: Auditory stimulus, auditory response

Have learners respond rapidly to questions such as, "Eight three?" (they respond, "Five"); "Eight four?" (they respond, "Four"); "Eight seven?" (they respond, "One"); and so on.

Engage them in this activity for four minutes per day, for the two consecutive lessons.

Activity #4: Visual stimulus, auditory response

Have learners respond rapidly and accurately when you tap 8–1, 8–2, 8–3, through 8–7 (vary the sequence through which you tap these facts) on the **Professor B Math Chart #2** (the Lower Subtraction Facts).

Engage them in this activity for four minutes per day, for the two consecutive lessons.

Activity #5: Visual stimulus, auditory response

Have learners respond rapidly and accurately when you tap 7+1, 6+2, 5+3, 4+4, 3+5, 2+6, and 1+7 (vary the sequence through which you tap these facts) on the **Professor B Math Chart #3** (the Lower Addition Facts).

Engage them in this activity for three minutes per day for the two consecutive lessons.

Activity #6: Class work and homework exercises

Immediately following the second lesson covering Activities #1 through #5, you must give learners class work, and afterward, assign homework involving a random mix of addition and subtraction (some horizontal, some vertical) using the facts in Activities #4 and #5 for the 10-, 9-, and 8-Charts.

Continue to give this type of class work and homework for the next six days.

These exercises are found in Workbook I.

Have learners practice the examples of Facility Exercises #26 through #33 (Workbook I) to the level of facility; **then move on**.

Activities #1 through #5 above must be done for the two lessons only.

Following these two lessons, they (the activities) must be replaced by the mixed practice activities described in the next section.

MIXED PRACTICE WITH THE 10-, 9-, AND 8-CHARTS

Objectives: The learners will

1. respond, instantly and accurately, with the complement in ten, nine, or eight, of any number chosen from one through nine, or one through eight, or one through seven, respectively, when given mixed practice involving all three;
2. respond, instantly and accurately, to symbolic representations of subtraction facts, in which the larger number is ten, nine, or eight, when given mixed practice involving all three; and,
3. respond, instantly and accurately, to symbolic representations of addition facts, for which the sum is ten, nine, or eight, when given mixed practice involving all three.

This mixed practice must be conducted at the beginning of every lesson for the next six days.

On these days, please remember to practice the recitation exercises for the 10-, 9-, and 8-Charts.

Activity #1: Auditory stimulus, auditory response

Have learners respond rapidly and accurately to questions such as, "Ten three?", "Nine five?", "Eight two?", "Nine one?", "Eight five?", "Ten six?", "Ten eight?", "Eight seven?", "Nine three?", and so on.

Try to catch them.

Engage them in this activity for four minutes per day for the first two of the six consecutive lessons.

Reduce the amount of time over the next four days.

Activity #2: Visual stimulus, auditory response

Have learners respond rapidly and accurately when you tap such sequences of facts as 10–6, 9–7, 8–6, 8–3, 10–8, 9–1, 9–4, 10–3, and 8–4 (vary the sequence through which you tap these facts) on the **Professor B Math Chart #2** (the Lower Subtraction Facts).

Try to catch them.

Engage them in this activity for four minutes per day for the first two of the six consecutive lessons.

Reduce the amount of time over the next four days.

Activity #3: Visual stimulus, auditory response

Have learners respond rapidly and accurately when you tap such sequences of facts as 5+5, 6+3, 8+2, 3+5, 7+2, 6+2, 1+9, 4+4, and 2+7 (vary the sequence through which you tap these facts) on the **Professor B Math Chart #3** (the Lower Addition Facts).

Try to catch them.

Engage them in this activity for four minutes per day, for the first two of the six consecutive lessons.

Reduce the amount of time over the next four days.

Activity #4: Class work and homework exercises

Continue (for the next six lessons) to assign mixed practice class work and homework, involving addition and subtraction (some horizontal, some vertical), using the facts from Activity #2 and #3 in this section.

MASTERING THE LOWER ADDITION AND SUBTRACTION FACTS: THE "SEVEN-CHART" GAME

Objectives: The learners will

1. respond, instantly and accurately, with the complement in seven, of any number chosen from one through six;
2. respond, instantly and accurately, to symbolic representations of subtraction facts, in which the larger number is seven; and,
3. respond, instantly and accurately, to symbolic representations of addition facts, for which the sum is seven.

For the next two or three lessons after you have practiced Activities #1 through #4 (mixed practice with the 10-, 9-, and 8-Charts), place the following on the board:

(7)	
6	1
5	2
4	3

Now ask the learners to fill in the numbers which they think belong on the 7-Chart.

Carefully follow the unison response activity instructions, as you lead your learners through the techniques of this section once per day, for two or three days.

For these two or three days, please **remember to practice Activities #1 through #4 for the 10-, 9-, and 8-Charts** (mixed practice), as well as the two recitation exercises for each of them, before working with the 7-Chart as described below.

Before you begin to work on the 7-Chart, it is **very important** that you "spell out" exactly the way in which you expect to catch them in the 7-Chart game: tell them they will forget they are working on seven and give you the responses for ten, nine, or eight.

Take the time to "rub it in"; you just can't wait to catch them thinking about ten, nine or eight, instead of seven.

If you do this well, you will be very surprised at the smooth transition from the 8-Chart to the 7-Chart.

Now proceed similarly as you did with the 8-Chart for two or three consecutive lessons (see below).

Step 1

With all learners looking intently on the 7-Chart (all the numbers in it), say any one of the numbers from one through six.

Learners must quickly respond with its complement in seven.

Continue with this rapid-response activity for 3 minutes.

Step 2

Gradually erase 1, 5, and 3 while tapping the empty spaces and having learners rapidly respond by saying the missing numbers.

This should take about 2 minutes.

Step 3

With half of the numbers missing, return to the original game (Step 1) in which you say any one of the numbers, from one through six, and learners respond accordingly.

Continue this for about 3 minutes.

Step 4

Resume the erasing (one at a time) and tapping of the empty spaces, while learners rapidly respond with the missing numbers.

Continue this until all numbers (except the 7) have been erased.

This should take about 3 minutes.

Step 5

With all the numbers missing, return, once more, to the original game (Step 1) in which you say one of the numbers, from one through six, and learners respond accordingly.

Continue this for about 3 minutes.

Repeat this entire 7-Chart game, starting from scratch, for one or two more lessons.

Remember to begin these lessons with a review of Activities #1 through #4 for the 10-, 9-, and 8-Charts (mixed practice), as well as the recitation exercises.

After these two or three lessons, learners must never see numbers in the 7-Chart again.

Learners will now have mastered the 7-Chart to the extent that they are able to instantly and accurately respond, with the complement in seven, of any number from one through six.

This mastery, once attained, will be sustained by means of the activities described below (remember that learners must never see numbers in the 7-, 8-, 9-, or 10-Charts again).

Conduct those activities with your learners for two consecutive lessons.

Please remember! Those activities (below) must be preceded by a review of Activities #1 through #4 for the 10-, 9-, and 8-Charts, as well as the two recitation exercises, for each of them.

Activity #1: First recitation exercise

Have each learner recite as follows: "Seven six, one; seven five, two; seven four, three; seven three, four; seven two, five; seven one, six."

Be sure learners practice this **daily,** until it has been mastered by all participants.

Activity #2: Second recitation exercise

Have each learner recite as follows: "Six one, seven; five two, seven; four three, seven; three four, seven; two five, seven; one six, seven."

Be sure learners practice this **daily,** until it has been mastered by all participants.

Activity #3: Auditory stimulus, auditory response

Have learners respond rapidly to questions such as, "Seven two?" (they respond, "Five"); "Seven four?" (they respond, "Three"); "Seven six?" (they respond, "One"); and so on.

Engage them in this activity for three minutes per day, for the two consecutive lessons.

Activity #4: Visual stimulus, auditory response

Have learners respond rapidly and accurately when you tap 7–1, 7–2, 7–3, through 7–6 (vary the sequence through which you tap these facts) on the **Professor B Math Chart #2** (the Lower Subtraction Facts).

Engage them in this activity for three minutes per day, for the two consecutive lessons.

Activity #5: Visual stimulus, auditory response

Have learners respond rapidly and accurately when you tap 6+1, 5+2, 4+3, 3+4, 2+5, and 1+6 (vary the sequence through which you tap these facts) on the **Professor B Math Chart #3** (the Lower Addition Facts).

Engage them in this activity for three minutes per day, for the two consecutive lessons.

Activity #6: Class work and homework exercises

Immediately following the second lesson covering Activities #1 through #5, you must give learners class work, and afterward, assign homework involving a random mix of addition and subtraction (some horizontal, some vertical), using the facts in Activities #4 and #5 for the 10-, 9-, 8-, and 7-Charts.

Continue to give this type of class work and homework for the next six days.

These exercises are found Workbook I.

Have learners practice the examples of Facility Exercises #34 through #41 (Workbook I) to the level of facility; **then move on**.

Activities #1 through #5 above must be done for two lessons only.

Following these two lessons, they (the activities) must be replaced by the mixed practice activities described in the next section.

MIXED PRACTICE WITH THE 10-, 9-, 8-, AND 7-CHARTS

Objectives: The learners will

1. respond, instantly and accurately, with the complement in ten, nine, eight or seven, of any number chosen from one through nine, one through eight, one through seven, or one through six, respectively, when given mixed practice involving all four;
2. respond, instantly and accurately, to symbolic representations of subtraction facts, in which the larger number is ten, nine, eight, or seven, when given mixed practice involving all four; and,
3. respond, instantly and accurately, to symbolic representations of addition facts, for which the sum is ten, nine, eight, or seven, when given mixed practice involving all four.

This mixed practice must be conducted at the beginning of every lesson for the next six days.

On these days, please remember to practice the recitation exercises for the 10-, 9-, 8-, and 7-Charts.

Activity #1: Auditory stimulus, auditory response

Have learners respond rapidly and accurately to questions such as, "Ten six?", "Nine three?", "Eight four?", "Seven five?", "Seven one?", "Nine four?", "Seven three?", "Eight two?", "Ten seven?", "Seven two?", "Nine seven?", and so on.

Try to catch them.

Engage them in this activity for four minutes per day for the first two of the six consecutive lessons.

Reduce the amount of time over the next four days.

Activity #2: Visual stimulus, auditory response

Have learners respond rapidly and accurately when you tap such sequences of facts as 10–4, 9–4, 8–2, 7–6, 9–7, 7–3, 10–5, 8–6, 7–5, 8–3, and 9–3 (vary the sequence through which you tap these facts) on the **Professor B Math Chart #2** (the Lower Subtraction Facts).

Try to catch them.

Engage them in this activity for four minutes per day for the first two of the six consecutive lessons.

Reduce the amount of time over the next four days.

Activity #3: Visual stimulus, auditory response

Have learners respond rapidly and accurately when you tap such sequences of facts as 6+4, 7+2, 5+3, 6+1, 4+3, 5+4, 9+1, 2+6, 4+4, 5+2, and 6+3 (vary the sequence through which you tap these facts) on the **Professor B Math Chart #3** (the Lower Addition Facts).

Try to catch them.

Engage them in this activity for four minutes per day, for the first two of the six consecutive lessons.

Reduce the amount of time over the next four days.

Activity #4: Class work and homework exercises

Continue (for the next six lessons) to assign mixed practice class work and homework, involving addition and subtraction (some horizontal, some vertical), using the facts from Activity #2 and #3 in this section.

MASTERING THE LOWER ADDITION AND SUBTRACTION FACTS: THE "SIX-CHART" GAME

Objectives: The learners will

1. respond, instantly and accurately, with the complement in six, of any number chosen from one through five;
2. respond, instantly and accurately, to symbolic representations of subtraction facts, in which the larger number is six; and,
3. respond, instantly and accurately, to symbolic representations of addition facts, for which the sum is six.

For the next two or three lessons after you have practiced Activities #1 through #4 (mixed practice with the 10-, 9-, 8-, and 7-Charts), place the following on the board:

6	
5	1
4	2
3	3

Now ask the learners to fill in the numbers which they think belong on the 6-Chart.

Carefully follow the unison response activity instructions, as you lead your learners through the techniques of this section once per day, for two or three days.

For these two or three days, **please remember to practice Activities #1 through #4 for the 10-, 9-, 8-, and 7-Charts** (mixed practice), as well as the two recitation exercises for each of them, before working with the 6-Chart as described below.

Before you begin to work on the 6-Chart, it is **very important** that you "spell out" exactly the way in which you expect to catch them in the 6-Chart game: tell them they will forget they are working on six and give you responses for ten, nine, eight, or seven.

If you do this well, you will be very surprised at the smooth transition from the 7-Chart to the 6-Chart.

Now proceed similarly, as you did with the 7-Chart, for two or three consecutive lessons (see below).

Step 1

With all learners looking intently on the 6-Chart (all the numbers in it), say any one of the numbers, from one through five.

Learners must quickly respond with its complement in six.

Continue with this rapid-response activity for 3 minutes.

Step 2

Gradually erase 1, 4, and 3 while tapping the empty spaces and having learners rapidly respond by saying the missing numbers.

This should take about 2 minutes.

Step 3

With half of the numbers missing, return to the original game (Step 1) in which you say any one of the numbers, from one through five, and learners respond accordingly.

Continue this for about 3 minutes.

Step 4

Resume the erasing (one at a time) and tapping of the empty spaces, while learners rapidly respond with the missing numbers.

Continue this until all numbers (except the 6) have been erased.

This should take about 3 minutes.

Step 5

With all the numbers missing, return, once more, to the original game (Step 1) in which you say any one of the numbers, from one through five, and learners respond accordingly.

Continue this for about 3 minutes.

Repeat the entire 6-Chart game, starting from scratch, for one or two more lessons.

Remember to begin these lessons with a review of Activities #1

through #4 for the 10-, 9-, 8-, and 7-Charts (mixed practice), as well as the recitation exercises.

After these two or three lessons, learners must never see numbers in the 6-Chart again.

Learners will now have mastered the 6-Chart to the extent that they are able to instantly and accurately respond, with the complement in six, of any number from one through five.

This mastery, once attained, will be sustained by means of the activities described below (remember that learners must never see numbers in the 6-, 7-, 8-, 9-, or 10-Charts again).

Conduct those activities with your learners for two consecutive lessons.

Please remember! Those activities (below) must be preceded by a review of Activities #1 through #4 for the 10-, 9-, 8-, and 7-Charts, as well as the two recitation exercises for each of them.

Activity #1: First recitation exercise

Have each learner recite as follows: "Six five, one; six four, two; six three, three; six three, three; six two, four; six one, five."

Be sure learners practice this **daily,** until it has been mastered by all participants.

Activity #2: Second recitation exercise

Have each learner recite as follows: "Five one, six; four two, six; three three, six; two four, six; one five, six."

Be sure learners practice this **daily,** until it has been mastered by all participants.

Activity #3: Auditory stimulus, auditory response

Have learners respond rapidly to questions such as, "Six two?" (they respond, "Four"); "Six five?" (they respond, "One"); "Six three?" (they respond, "Three"); and so on.

Engage them in this activity for three minutes per day, for the two consecutive lessons.

Activity #4: Visual stimulus, auditory response

Have learners respond rapidly and accurately when you tap 6–1, 6–2, 6–3, 6–4, and 6–5 (vary the sequence through which you tap these facts) on the **Professor B Math Chart #2** (the Lower Subtraction Facts).

Engage them in this activity for three minutes per day, for the two consecutive lessons.

Activity #5: Visual stimulus, auditory response

Have learners respond, rapidly and accurately, when you tap 5+1, 4+2, 3+3, 3+3, 2+4, and 1+5 (vary the sequence through which you tap these facts) on the **Professor B Math Chart #3** (the Lower Addition Facts). Engage them in this activity for three minutes per day, for the two consecutive lessons.

Activity #6: Class work and homework exercises

Immediately following the second lesson covering Activities #1 through #5, you must give learners class work, and afterward, assign homework involving a random mix of addition and subtraction (some horizontal, some vertical), using the facts in Activities #4 and #5 for the 10-, 9-, 8-, 7-, and 6-Charts.

Continue to give this type of class work and homework for the next six days.

These exercises are found in Workbook I.

Have learners practice the examples of Facility Exercises #42 through #49 (Workbook I) to the level of facility; **then move on**.

Activities #1 through #5 above must be done for two lessons only.

Following these two lessons, they (the activities) must be replaced by the mixed practice activities described in the next section.

MIXED PRACTICE WITH THE 10-, 9-, 8-, 7-, AND 6-CHARTS

Objectives: The learners will

1. respond, instantly and accurately, with the complement in ten, nine, eight, seven, or six, of any number chosen from one through nine, one through eight, one through seven, one through six, or one through five, respectively, when given mixed practice involving all five;
2. respond, instantly and accurately, to symbolic representations of subtraction facts, in which the larger number is ten, nine, eight, seven, or six, when given mixed practice involving all five; and,
3. respond, instantly and accurately, to symbolic representations of addition facts, for which the sum is ten, nine, eight, seven, or six, when given mixed practice involving all five.

This mixed practice must be conducted at the beginning of every lesson for the next six days.

On these days, please remember to practice the recitation exercises.

Activity #1: Auditory stimulus, auditory response

Have learners respond rapidly and accurately to questions such as, "Ten six?", "Six four?", "Seven two?", "Ten eight?", "Six five?", "Eight two?", "Seven one?", "Nine seven?", "Six three?", and so on.

Try to catch them.

Engage them in this activity for four minutes per day for the first two of the six consecutive lessons.

Reduce the amount of time over the next four days.

Activity #2: Visual stimulus, auditory response

Have learners respond rapidly and accurately when you tap such sequences of facts as 10–6, 6–4, 7–2, 8–5, 6–2, 9–6, 7–3, 10–8, 6–5, 8–2, 7–1, 9–7, and 6–3 (vary the sequence through which you tap these facts) on the **Professor B Math Chart #2** (the Lower Subtraction Facts).

Try to catch them.

Engage them in this activity for four minutes per day, for the first two of the six consecutive lessons.

Reduce the amount of time over the next four days.

Activity #3: Visual stimulus, auditory response

Have learners respond, rapidly and accurately, when you tap such sequences of facts as 6+4, 4+2, 2+5, 5+3, 3+3, 6+3, 4+3, 8+2, 5+1, 2+6, 6+1, 7+2, and 5+2 (vary the sequence through which you tap these facts) on the **Professor B Math Chart #3** (the Lower Addition Facts).

Try to catch them.

Engage them in this activity for four minutes per day, for the first two of the six consecutive lessons.

Reduce the amount of time over the next four days.

Activity #4: Class work and homework exercises

Continue (for the next six lessons) to assign mixed practice class work and homework, involving addition and subtraction (some horizontal, some vertical), using the facts from Activity #2 and #3 in this section.

MASTERING THE LOWER ADDITION AND SUBTRACTION FACTS: THE FIVE-, FOUR-, THREE-, AND TWO-CHART GAMES

Objectives: The learners will

1. respond, instantly and accurately, with the complement in five, four, three, or two, of any counting number less than itself;
2. respond, instantly and accurately, to symbolic representations of subtraction facts, in which the larger number is five, four, three, or two; and,
3. respond, instantly and accurately, to symbolic representations of addition facts for which the sum is five, four, three, or two.

For the next two or three lessons after you have practiced Activities #1 through #4 (mixed practice with the 10-, 9-, 8-, 7-, and 6-Charts), place the following on the board:

(5)	
4	1
3	2

(4)	
3	1
2	2

(3)	
2	1

(2)	
1	1

Now ask the learners to fill in the numbers which they think belong on the 5-, 4-, 3-, and 2-Charts.

Carefully follow the unison response activity instructions, as you lead your learners through the techniques of this section once per day, for two or three days.

For these two or three days, **please remember to practice Activities #1 through #4 for the 10-, 9-, 8-, 7-, and 6-Charts** (mixed practice), as well as the two recitation exercises, before working with the 5-, 4-, 3-, and 2-Charts as described below.

At this point, apply Step 1 through Step 5 to the 5-Chart.

During the same lesson, apply Step 1 through Step 5 to the 4-, 3-, and 2-Charts.

Repeat this activity for two more lessons.

Remember to begin these lessons with a review of Activities #1 through #4 for the 10-, 9-, 8-, 7-, and 6-Charts (mixed practice), as well as the two recitation exercises.

After these three lessons, learners must never see numbers in the 5-, 4-, 3-, and 2-Charts again.

Learners will now have mastered the 5-, 4-, 3-, and 2-Charts, to the extent that they are able to instantly and accurately respond with

1. the complement in five, of any number from one through four;
2. the complement in four, of any number from one through three;
3. the complement in three, of one or two; and
4. the complement in two of one.

This mastery, once attained, will be sustained by means of the activities described below (remember that learners must never see numbers in the 5-, 4-, 3-, and 2-Charts again).

Conduct these activities with your learners for two consecutive lessons (over two days).

Activity #1: First recitation exercise

Have each learner recite as shown below.

1. "Five four, one; five three, two; five two, three; five one, four."
2. "Four three, one; four two, two; four two, two; four one, three."
3. "Three two, one; three one, two."
4. "Two one, one."

Be sure learners practice this **daily** until it has been mastered by all participants.

Activity #2: Second recitation exercise

Have each learner recite as shown below.

1. "Four one, five; three two, five; two three, five; one four, five."
2. "Three one, four; two two, four; two two, four; one three, four."
3. "Two one, three; one two, three."
4. "One one, two."

Be sure learners practice this **daily,** until it has been mastered by all participants.

Activity #3: Auditory stimulus, auditory response

Have learners respond rapidly to questions, such as those which follow below:

1. "Five four?" (they respond, "One"); "Five three?" (they respond, "Two"); and so on.
2. "Four two?" (they respond, "Two"); "Four one?" (they respond, "Three"); and so on.
3. "Three one?" (they respond, "Two"); "Three two?" (they respond, "One").
4. "Two one?" (they respond, "One").

Engage them in this activity for three minutes per day, for two consecutive lessons.

Activity #4: Visual stimulus, auditory response

Have learners respond, rapidly and accurately, when you tap (on the **Professor B Math Chart #2**) as follows below:

1. 5–1, 5–2, 5–3, and 5–4;
2. 4–1, 4–2, and 4–3;
3. 3–1 and 3–2; and
4. 2–1.

Vary the sequence through which you tap these facts.

Engage them in this activity for three minutes per day, for two consecutive lessons.

Activity #5: Visual stimulus, auditory response

Have learners respond, rapidly and accurately, when you tap on the **Professor B Math Chart #3** as follows below:

1. 4+1, 3+2, 2+3, and 1+4;
2. 3+1, 2+2, and 1+3;
3. 2+1 and 1+2; and
4. 1+1.

Vary the sequence through which you tap these facts.

Engage them in this activity for three minutes per day, for two consecutive lessons.

Activity #6: Class work and homework exercises

Immediately following the second lesson concerning Activities #1 through #5, you must give learners class work and, afterward, assign homework involving a random mix of addition and subtraction (some horizontal, some vertical) using the facts in Activities #4 and #5 for the 10-, 9-, 8-, 7-, 6-, 5-, 4-, 3-, and 2-Charts.

Continue to give this type of class work and homework for the next six days.

These exercises are found in Workbook I.

Have learners practice the examples of Facility Exercises #50 through #57 (Workbook I) to the level of facility; **then move on**.

Activities #1 through #5 above must be done for two lessons only.

Following these two lessons, they (the activities) must be replaced by the mixed practice activities described in the next section.

MIXED PRACTICE WITH ALL THE CHARTS

Objectives: The learners will

1. respond, instantly and accurately, with the complement in ten, nine, eight, seven, six, five, four, three, or two, of any counting number less than itself, when given mixed practice involving them all;
2. respond, instantly and accurately, to symbolic representations of subtraction facts, in which the larger number is ten, nine, eight, seven, six, five, four, three, or two, when given mixed practice involving all of them; and,
3. respond, instantly and accurately, to symbolic representations of addition facts, for which the sum is ten, nine, eight, seven, six, five, four, three, or two, when given mixed practice involving all of them.

This mixed practice must be conducted at the beginning of every lesson for the next six days.

Activity #1: Auditory stimulus, auditory response

Have learners respond rapidly and accurately to questions such as "Six two?", "Five three?", "Two one?", "Ten seven?", "Four two?", "Seven four?", "Six three?", "Eight three?", "Five one?", "Three one?", "Nine six?", "Six two?", and so on.

Try to catch them.

Engage them in this activity for four minutes per day, for the six consecutive lessons.

Activity #2: Visual stimulus, auditory response

Have learners respond rapidly and accurately when you tap such sequences as 6–4, 5–2, 2–1, 10–7, 4–2, 7–4, 6–3, 8–3, 5–1, 3–1, 9–6, and 6—3 (vary the sequence) on the **Professor B Math Chart #2**.

Try to catch them.

Engage them in this activity for four minutes per day, for the six consecutive lessons.

Activity #3: Visual stimulus, auditory response

Have learners respond rapidly and accurately when you tap such sequences as 4+2, 2+3, 1+1, 3+7, 2+2, 4+3, 3+3, 5+3, 1+4, 2+1, 3+6, 1+3, and 7+2 (vary the sequence) on the **Professor B Math Chart #3**.

Try to catch them.

Engage them in this activity for four minutes per day, for the six consecutive lessons.

Activity #4: Class work and homework exercises

Continue to assign mixed practice class work and homework, involving addition and subtraction (some horizontal, some vertical), using the facts from Activities #2 and #3 in this section.

After six lessons, reduce the daily time spent on Activities #2 and #3.

However, since mastery, once attained, must be sustained, it is necessary to continue this practice on a **daily** basis.

COUNTING TO 100 AND BEYOND

Objective: The learners will count from one to one hundred and beyond.

Teach learners to count to one hundred by means of the chart below (**Professor B Math Chart #4**).

1	2	3	4	5	6	7	8	9
10	20	30	40	50	60	70	80	90

Learners will have skill in counting to 100, after practicing to facility in each of the four phases below.

Phase 1

In this phase of the process toward counting from 1 to 100, learners are to say **nothing,** while doing the "tapping" described below.

Have a learner take a pointer and tap (on the chart) 1, then 2, then 3, then 4, and so on, up to 10.

After tapping 10, have the learner **pause briefly,** and continue as follows: tap 10 and 1, then 10 and 2, then 10 and 3, and so on, up to 10 and 9.

Tapping 10 and 9 is followed by tapping 20.

Have the learner **pause briefly** at 20, and continue tapping as follows: 20 and 1, 20 and 2, 20 and 3, and so on, up to 20 and 9.

Tapping 20 and 9 is followed by tapping 30.

Have the learner **pause briefly** at 30, and continue tapping: 30 and 1, 30 and 2, and so on, up to 30 and 9.

The tapping continues similarly through the 40's, 50's, 60's, up to the 90's.

Be sure the learner **pauses** at 40 (50, 60, 70, 80, 90) before tapping 40 and 1 (50 and 1, 60 and 1, 70 and 1, 80 and 1, 90 and 1).

Eventually, the learner will tap 90 and 9.

Clearly, it is inadvisable to ask one child to tap all the way from one to ninety-nine.

Consequently, each learner must have much practice in tapping out various parts of the sequence: for example, 1 to 32, or 8 to 40, or 13 to 44, or 26 to 54, and so on.

Phase 2

After they have facility with tapping, learners can begin to tap and talk simultaneously.

As 1 through 9 are tapped, a learner can say, "one" through "nine."

The learner taps 10, says the word "ten," and pauses.

Tapping 10 and 1 through 10 and 9, the learner says the words, "eleven" through "nineteen."

The learner taps 20, says the word "twenty," and pauses.

Tapping 20 and 1 through 20 and 9, the learner says the words "twenty-one" through "twenty-nine."

The learner taps 30, says the word "thirty," and pauses.

Continuing similarly, learners will "tap-talk" until they get to "ninety-nine."

Tell learners that after ninety-nine they say, "one hundred."

Each learner must have much practice in tap-talking various parts of the sequence.

Phase 3

In this phase, the tapping stops and the talking continues.

Have learners practice saying various parts of the counting sequence, from one to one hundred, while only looking at the chart.

Phase 4

The learners must practice saying various parts of the counting sequence, without looking at the chart.

Have learners practice the examples of Facility Exercises #58 (Workbook I) to the level of facility; **then move on.** Please note: this activity is **oral**.

Now that the learners can count from 1 to 100, they can learn to count from 101 to 200.

Tell learners to count from 1 to 99; but have them say, "One hundred" before each numeral.

As a result of this activity, learners will say, "One hundred one, one hundred two, one hundred three," and so on, up to "one hundred ninety-nine."

Tell learners that after 199 comes 200.

Have learners count from 1 to 99; but have them say, "two hundred" before each numeral.

In this way, they count from 201 to 299. Tell learners that after 299 comes 300.

By means of the above procedure, have learners count from 301 to 400; from 401 to 500; from 501 to 600; from 601 to 700; from 701 to 800; from 801 to 900; from 901 to 999.

Tell learners that after 999 comes 1,000.

Have learners practice the examples of Facility Exercises #59 (Workbook I) to the level of facility; **then move on.** Please note: this activity is **oral.**

If learners can say, "One, two, three, four, five," and so on, up to "nine hundred ninety-nine"; then they can say, "one thousand" before each numeral, and they will be counting, "One thousand one, one thousand two, one thousand three, one thousand four," and so on, up to one thousand nine hundred ninety-nine.

By saying "two thousand" first, learners will be counting from two thousand one, to two thousand nine hundred ninety-nine.

Similarly, learners can count from three thousand one, to three thousand nine hundred ninety-nine, from four thousand one, to four thousand nine hundred ninety-nine; and so on, up to counting from nine thousand one, to nine thousand nine hundred ninety-nine.

Please note the author is **not** suggesting learners be asked to count from 1 to 999, or from 1,001 to 1,999, or from 2,001 to 2,999, and so on.

The author can count to 1,000,000, but has never done it.

To say learners can count from 1,001 to 1,999 means they "know how" to do it.

Ask,

"What is 999+1?" (We have already said that 999 and one more makes one thousand)

"So what is 1,999+1? 2,999+1? 3,999+1? 4,999+1? 6,999+1? 8,999+1? 5,999+1? 7,999+1?"

Below are some counting exercises you can ask individual learners to perform:

1. Count from 1,041 to 1,063.
2. Count from 8,673 to 8,698.
3. Count from 2,489 to 2,509.
4. Count from 6,983 to 7,015.

Have learners practice the examples of Facility Exercises #60 (Workbook I) to the level of facility; **then move on.** Please note: this activity is **oral**.

Learners should be given sufficient practice counting various quantities of objects. The quantity of objects may not exceed one hundred.

VOCABULARY AND SYMBOLISM OF NUMERATION

Objective: Learners will read numerals up to "the trillions."

Write the numerals 10, 20, 30, 40, 50, 60, 70, 80, 90 on the board.

Tell learners that "70" says "seventy."

Ask the following questions:
"What does '80' say? '60'? '40'? '90'?"
"What does '50' say?"
Beginners may say "fivety" for 50.

Inform learners that people say "fifty" for 50.

You may have similarly elicited "threety" for 30, "twoty" for 20, and "onety" for 10.

Have learners say "thirty" in place of threety; "twenty" in place of twoty; and "ten" in place of onety.

Have learners practice the above to the level of facility; **then move on.**

Write the following on the board:

27,	29,	24,	26,	21,	23
34,	47,	53,	67,	73,	94

Tell learners that "27" says " twenty-seven."

Ask the following questions:

"What does '29' say? '24'? '26'? '23'? '34'? '47'? '53'? '67'? '73'? '85'? '94'?"

Have learners practice reading the two digit numerals in Facility Exercises #61 (Workbook I) to the level of facility; **then move on.** Please note: this activity is **oral**.

Have learners recall that, in the process of learning to count, they pointed to "10" and then to "7" (on the chart) and said, "Seventeen."

Tell learners that seventeen comes from seven and ten; so "teen" means ten.

Ask, "Can you hear seven and teen in seventeen?"

You should now write 17 on the board and, pointing to the 7, say, "Seven" and to the 1 (in 17), say, "Teen," (which means ten).

Similarly, ask learners what each of the digits says in 14, 16, 18, and 19.

In this manner, the learners will have named 14, 16, 18, and 19.

Example:

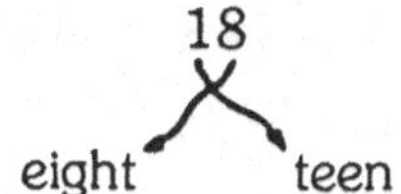

Write 13 on the board.

Point to it and ask, "How would you read this?" Based on what has been done so far, learners may answer, "Threeteen" (which means three and ten).

Remind them that when learning to count with the chart (see page 68), they pointed to 10, and then to 3, and said, "Thirteen."

Tell them that thirteen is the accepted way to read "13."

Based on what has been done so far, learners may say, "Fiveteen" for 15;

"Twoteen" for 12; and "Oneteen" for 11.

The commonly used names for 11, 12, and 15, can be elicited in the same way as was done for 13.

Take 12, for example.

Remind learners that when counting with the chart, they pointed to 10 and 2 then said, "Twelve."

Tell them that "twelve" is the accepted way to read "12."

Have learners practice the above to the level of facility: **then move on.**

Write 647 on the board.

Tell learners that anyone who can read 47 can also read 647.
"The '6' on the left of 647 says, 'six hundred'."
"So 647 says, 'six hundred forty seven'."

Write 547 on the board.

Ask learners, "How would you read 547?"

Write the following on the board:

247 947 847 747 147 347 447

Have learners read each of the above numerals.

Write 468 on the board.

Tell learners that anyone who can read 68 can also read 468.

Write the following on the board:

568 268 968 368 768 868 168 668

Have learners read each of the above numerals.

Write 318 on the board.

Tell learners that anyone who can read 18 can also read 318.

Write the following on the board:

718 518 918 218 418 618 118 818

Have learners read each of the above numerals.

Write 511 on the board.

Tell learners that anyone who can read 11 can also read 511.

Write the following on the board:

811 311 711 411 111 611 211 911

Have learners read each of the above numerals.

Have learners practice reading the three digit numerals in Facility Exercises #62 (Workbook I) to the level of facility; **then move on.** Please note: this activity is **oral**.

Write 697 on the board.

Tell the learners to look and listen to you very carefully.

Take a pointer, touch the digit 6 and say, "Six hundred"; then touch the digit 9 and say, "Ninety"; then touch the digit 7 and say, "Seven."

Now touch the digit 6 and ask the learners, "What does this say?"

They respond, "Six hundred."

Touch the digit 9 and ask, "What does this say?"

They respond, "Ninety."

Touch the digit 7 and ask, "What does this say?"

They respond, "Seven."

From this point onward, for the next minute, rapidly and **randomly** tap the digits 6, 9, and 7, as the learners respond appropriately.

Be sure that you do not keep tapping in a particular sequence.

Try to surprise them.

For example, in one sequence, you could tap the 9 first; then the 7; then the 6.

Learners would respond, "Ninety"; then, "Seven"; then, "Six hundred."

At this point, you must write 769 on the board under 697. See Below.

697
769

In the left column, tap 6 and ask, "What does this say?"

Now tap 7 in the left column and say, "Seven hundred."

In the middle column, tap 9 and ask, "What does this say?"

Now tap 6 in the middle column and say, "Sixty."

In the right column, tap 7 and ask, "What does this say?"

Now tap 9 in the right column and say, "Nine." At this point, rapidly and **randomly** tap among the six digits, for about one minute, as the learners respond appropriately.

Now write 976 on the board under the other two numerals.

697
769
976

In the left column,

1. tap 6 (learners respond, "Six hundred"),
2. tap 7 (learners respond, "Seven hundred"), and
3. tap 9 (learners respond, "Nine hundred").

In the middle column,

1. tap 9 (learners respond, "Ninety"),
2. tap 6 (learners respond, "Sixty"), and
3. tap 7 (learners respond, "Seventy").

In the right column,

1. tap 7 (learners respond, "Seven"),
2. tap 9 (learners respond, "Nine"), and
3. tap 6 (learners respond, "Six").

At this point, rapidly and **randomly** tap among the nine digits, for about two minutes, as the learners respond appropriately.

Now write 385 on the board under the other three numbers.

697
769
976
385

In the middle column, tap 8 (learners respond, "Eighty").

In the right column, tap 5 (learners respond, "Five").

In the left column, tap 3 (learners respond, "Three hundred").

At this point, rapidly and **randomly** tap among the twelve digits, for about two minutes, as the learners respond appropriately.

Finally, write 538 on the board under the other four numbers.

697
769
976
385
538

Rapidly and **randomly** tap among the fifteen digits for two to three minutes, as the learners respond appropriately.

At this point, you should write the five numbers horizontally on the board, with spaces between them as appears below:

697 769 976 385 538

With the five numbers arranged in this manner, rapidly and **randomly** tap among the fifteen digits for two to three minutes, as the learners respond appropriately (they will make the same responses as above).

Now place commas in the spaces between the numbers as follows:

697 , 769 , 976 , 385 , 538

trillion billion million thousand

Tell the learners that the commas are given names:

1. The name of the first comma starting from the right is "thousand."
2. The name of the second comma from the right is "million."
3. The name of the third comma from the right is "billion."
4. The name of the fourth comma from the right is "trillion."

For about two minutes, tap the various commas rapidly and randomly, while learners practice at naming them quickly and accurately.

Tell the learners, "Follow the pointer."

Be sure that no child goes ahead of, or lags behind, the pointer.

As you move, from left to right, across the number, tapping the digits and the commas, the learners will say, "Six hundred ninety-seven trillion, seven hundred sixty-nine billion, nine hundred seventy-six million, three hundred eighty-five thousand, five hundred thirty-eight."

697	,	769	,	976	,	385	,	538
six hundred ninety-seven		seven hundred sixty-nine		nine hundred seventy-six		three hundred eighty-five		five hundred thirty-eight
	trillion		billion		million		thousand	

This whole lesson, from the moment you first wrote 697 on the board, to the reading of the number in the previous paragraph, should take about twenty minutes.

Have learners practice reading the numerals in Facility Exercises #63 (Workbook I) to the level of facility: **then move on.**

Write the following on the board:

600,005,070,380,502

Tell the learners, "We are going to play a new game. The name of this game is **'the zeros are silent.'** I repeat! The zeros are silent."

As you move, from left to right, across the number, tapping the digits and the commas, the learners should be absolutely silent whenever you tap a zero.

Hence they will say, "Six hundred trillion, five billion, seventy million, three hundred eighty thousand, five hundred two."

Have learners practice reading the numerals in Facility Exercises #64 (Workbook I) to the level of facility: **then move on.**

Write the following on the board:

190,000,100,000,001
201,000,000,200,000

Tell the learners, "Here's another game. In this game, **a comma is silent** if it has three zeros on its left. Now look at the first number and see if you can find commas with three zeros on their left; but don't tell anyone about it."

Now as you move from left to right across the first number, tapping the digits and commas, the learners should not only be absolutely silent when you tap a zero; they must also be silent when you tap the billions' and thousands' commas.

Hence they will say, "One hundred ninety trillion, one hundred million, one."

They will read the second number as follows: "Two hundred one trillion, two hundred thousand."

Have learners practice reading the numerals in Facility Exercises #65 (Workbook I) to the level of facility: **then move on.**

Inform the learners as follows:

1. If the numeral has one comma, the name of that comma is thousand.
2. If the numeral has two commas, the name of the first comma on the right is thousand, and the name of the second comma from the right is million.
3. If the numeral has three commas, the name of the first comma on the right is thousand; the name of the second comma from the right is million; and the name of the third comma from the right is billion.

Write the following on the board:

231,428
518,264,709
423,089,043,278

Have the learners read these numerals.

Write the following numerals on the board:

1
10
100
1,000
10,000
100,000
1,000,000
10,000,000
100,000,000
1,000,000,000
10,000,000,000
100,000,000,000
1,000,000,000,000

Have the learners read these numerals.

Have learners practice reading the numerals in Facility Exercises #66 (Workbook I) to the level of facility: **then move on.**

FOR THE APPRECIATION OF THE METHOD FOR ADDING LARGE NUMBERS

Objective: Learners will ask you to teach them the method for adding two large numbers.

Write on the board:

$$\begin{array}{r} 3 \\ +\ \underline{2} \end{array}$$

Have the learners arrive at the answer to the above example by gathering a set of three objects and a set of two objects, then counting the total (five objects).

Write on the board:

$$\begin{array}{r} 7 \\ +\ \underline{5} \end{array}$$

Have the learners arrive at the answer to the above example by gathering a set of seven objects and a set of five objects, then counting the total (twelve objects).

Write on the board:

$$\begin{array}{r} 18 \\ +\ \underline{14} \end{array}$$

Ask the learners to find the answer to the problem on the board by gathering the two sets of objects, and counting the total (thirty-two objects).

Write on the board:

$$\begin{array}{r} 35 \\ +\ \underline{29} \end{array}$$

Ask the learners to find the answer to the problem on the board by gathering the two sets of objects, and counting the total (sixty-four objects).

Write on the board:

$$\begin{array}{r} 5{,}342 \\ +\ \underline{3{,}254} \end{array}$$

Try not to laugh, or even smile (it will be difficult) as you request that the learners find the answer to the problem on the board by gathering the two sets of objects, and counting the total.

Remain silent for a while and listen carefully to the expressions of their concerns and complaints.

You might facilitate the articulation of their concerns by asking such questions as, "Why don't you do this problem in the same way you did the others?" and, "How long do you think it would take to find the answer?"

Ask the learners, "Would you want to take a very 'lo-o-ong' time to finish this problem, or would you like to learn a short-cut which would take less than one minute?"

Tell the learners that the short-cut for adding larger numbers is called the addition algorithm.

Emphasize that the addition algorithm is a short-cut.

Now ask, "Do you want to learn the addition algorithm?" (All learners say, "YES!")

Tell learners they will be using the addition algorithm to add very large numbers (like those on the board) in the near future.

ADDING TWO LARGE WHOLE NUMBERS
(without regrouping)

Objectives: The learners will

(a) add any two whole numbers up to "the billions" without regrouping; and,

(b) respond, quickly and accurately, to questions involving the lower addition facts.

In this section, we will give learners intensive practice on addition examples (no regrouping), with numbers which go up to the billions.

By doing many of these, learners will continue to strengthen their power to instantly and accurately recall the lower addition facts.

The use of long additions as a vehicle for attaining quick mental recall of addition facts permits learners to acquire both skills simultaneously.

At this point, we will not have the learners involved with place value as they do long additions.

It is sufficient, for now, that they concentrate on the skill of adding large numbers, without regrouping.

After they have done an example, you must ask learners to read the top numeral, the bottom numeral, and the answer.

This provides some involvement with place value. As you will see later, the ability to read large numerals is related to the determination of place value.

Write the following on the board:

$$\begin{array}{r} 4{,}250{,}371{,}642 \\ + \underline{\quad 339{,}325{,}336} \end{array}$$

Have learners copy this example.

Be sure each learner takes great pains to place digits in the bottom numeral "right under" corresponding digits in the top numeral.

Do not be concerned when learners' first attempts at writing such long addition examples are somewhat clumsy. This is normal.

With **daily** practice at writing long additions, **all learners** inevitably improve.

Tell learners, "When I touch it, you say it."

Starting on the right, touch the digit 2. Learners say, "Two."

Touch the plus sign. Learners say, "Plus."

Touch the digit 6. Learners say, "Six."

Ask, "What are 2 plus 6?"

Tell learners, "Write the 8 right under the 6."

Touch the digit 4 in the next column. Learners say, "Four."

Touch the plus sign. Learners say, "Plus."

Touch the digit 3. Learners say, "Three."

Ask, "What are 4 plus 3?"

Tell learners, "Write the 7 right under the 3."

Continue similarly up to the hundred millions' column.

Now touch the digit 4 in the last column. Learners say, "Four."

Touch the plus sign. Learners say, "Plus."

Touch the blank space beneath the 4. Have learners say, "Nothing."

Ask, "What are 4 plus nothing?"

Tell learners, "Write the 4 right under the 4."

Be sure to have learners "bring down" the commas.

Have each learner look at the completed example and read the result as follows:

"Four billion, two hundred fifty million, three hundred seventy-one thousand, six hundred forty-two plus three hundred thirty-nine million,three hundred twenty-five thousand, three hundred thirty-six equals four billion, five hundred eighty-nine million, six hundred ninety-six thousand, nine hundred seventy-eight."

Have learners copy each example below and elicit responses as done above.

After completing each example, have learners look at it, and read the result (as in the above example).

(a)
$$\begin{array}{r} 361{,}425{,}342 \\ +\underline{7{,}238{,}453{,}135} \end{array}$$

(b)
$$\begin{array}{r} 506{,}372{,}145 \\ +\underline{392{,}320{,}124} \end{array}$$

(c)
$$\begin{array}{r} 2{,}538{,}146{,}205 \\ +\underline{7{,}250{,}733{,}792} \end{array}$$

Learners should now attempt to do the exercises below by themselves.

Be sure they **start on the right**.

Have learners practice the examples of Facility Exercises #67 (Workbook I) to the level of facility: **then move on.**

PLACE VALUE

Objectives: The learners will name

(a) the number which each digit in any large numeral up to the trillions represents; and,

(b) the value of any place within any large numeral up to the trillions.

Write the following on the board:

385,271,436,954,278

Take a pointer and tell the learners to say what you touch.

Insist that learners **"follow the pointer."**

The success of this lesson requires that no learner either goes ahead of, or falls behind the others.

Point to the digit 3 (first 3 from the left).

Learners say, "Three hundred."

Now point immediately to the trillions' comma.

Learners say, "Trillion."

Have learners respond once again as you tap the three, and then the trillions' comma.

Learners respond, "Three hundred trillion."

At this point, you must say, "This digit represents the number three hundred trillion."

Point to the digit 3 again and ask, "What number does this digit represent?"

Learners respond appropriately.

Point to the digit 2 (first 2 from the left) and ask, "What number does this digit represent?"

Learners respond, "Two hundred billion."

Point to the digit 4 (first 4 from the left) and ask, "What number does this digit represent?"

Learners respond, "Four hundred million."

Point to the digit 9 and ask, "What number does this digit represent?"

Learners respond, "Nine hundred thousand."

Point to the digit 2 (second 2 from the left) and ask, "What number does this digit represent?"

Learners respond, "Two hundred."

Point to the digit 8 (first 8 from the left) and ask, "What number does this digit represent?"

Learners respond, "Eighty trillion."

Point to the digit 7 (first 7 from the left) and ask, "What number does this digit represent?"

Learners respond, "Seventy billion."

Point to the digit 3 (second 3 from the left) and ask, "What number does this digit represent?"

Learners respond, "Thirty million."

Point to the digit 5 (second 5 from the left) and ask, "What number does this digit represent?"

Learners respond, "Fifty thousand."

Point to the digit 7 (second 7 from the left) and ask, "What number does this digit represent?"

Learners respond, "Seventy."

Point to the digit 5 (first 5 from the left) and ask, "What number does this digit represent?"

Learners respond, "Five trillion."

Point to the digit 1 and ask, "What number does this digit represent?"

Learners respond, "One billion."

Point to the digit 6 and ask, "What number does this digit represent?"

Learners respond, "Six million."

Point to the digit 4 (second 4 from the left) and ask, "What number does this digit represent?"

Learners respond, "Four thousand."

Point to the digit 8 (second 8 from the left) and ask, "What number does this digit represent?"

Learners respond, "Eight."

Have learners practice this activity by pointing to different digits in each numeral below, and asking each time, "What number does this digit represent?"

Write the following on the board:

257,428,345,942,584
72,495,186

Have learners practice the examples of Facility Exercises #68 (Workbook I) to the level of facility: **then move on.** Please note: this activity is **oral.**

Write the following on the board:

473,984,265,174,893

Point to the digit 4 (first 4 from the left) and ask, "What number does this digit represent?"

Learners respond, "Four hundred trillion."

Tell them to repeat this while listening carefully to their own voices.

Now tell them to repeat it again, but this time just leave out the word "four." Learners respond, "Hundred trillion."

Tell learners, "This is the hundred trillions' place."

Now ask, "What place is this?"

Learners respond, "Hundred trillions' place."

Point to the digit 9 (first 9 from the left) and ask, "What number does this digit represent?"

Learners respond, "Nine hundred billion."

Tell them to repeat this while listening to their own voices.

Now tell them to repeat it again, but this time just leave out the word "nine."

Learners respond, "Hundred billion."

Tell learners, "This is the hundred-billions' place."

Now ask, "What place is this?"

Learners respond, "Hundred-billions' place."

Point to the digit 2 and ask, "What place is this?"

Learners respond, "Hundred-millions' place."

Point to the digit 1 and ask, "What place is this?"

Learners respond, "Hundred-thousands' place."

Point to the digit 8 (second 8 from the left) and ask, "What place is this?"

Learners respond, "Hundreds' place."

Now point to the digit 7 (first 7 from the left) and ask, "What number does this digit represent?"

Learners respond, "Seventy trillion."

Tell them to repeat this while listening to their own voices.

Now tell them to repeat it again, but this time they must drop the sound "ty" and put "ten" in its place.

Learners respond, "Seven ten trillion."

Tell them to repeat what they just said, while listening to their own voices.

Now have them repeat it again, but this time just leave out the word "seven."

Learners respond, "Ten trillion."

Tell learners, "This is the ten-trillions' place."

Now ask, "What place is this?"

Learners respond, "Ten-trillions' place."

Now point to the digit 8 (first 8 from the left) and ask, "What number does this digit represent?"

Learners respond, "Eighty billion."

Tell them to repeat this while listening to their own voices.

Now tell them to repeat it again, but this time they must drop the sound "ty" and put "ten" in its place.

Learners respond, "Eight ten billion."

Tell them to repeat what they just said, while listening to their own voices.

Now have them repeat it again, but this time just leave out the word "eight."

Learners respond, "Ten billion."

Tell learners, "This is the ten-billions' place."

Now ask, "What place is this?"

Learners respond, "Ten-billions' place."

Point to the digit 6 and ask, "What place is this?"

Learners respond, "Ten-millions' place."

Point to the digit 7 (second 7 from the left) and ask, "What place is this?"

Learners respond, "Ten-thousands' place."

Point to the digit 9 (second 9 from the left) and ask, "What place is this?"

Learners respond, "Tens' place."

Now point to the digit 3 (first 3 from the left) and ask, "What number does this digit represent?"

Learners respond, "Three trillion."

Tell them to repeat it, but this time just leave out the word "three."

Learners respond, "Trillion."

Tell learners, "This is the trillions' place." Now ask, "What place is this?"

Learners respond, "Trillions' place."

Now point to the digit 4 (second 4 from the left) and ask, "What place is this?"

Learners respond, "Billions' place."

Point to the digit 5 and ask, "What place is this?"

Learners respond, "Millions' place."

Point to the digit 4 (third 4 from the left) and ask, "What place is this?"

Learners respond, "Thousands' place."

Point to the digit 3 (second 3 from the left) and ask, "What place is this?"

Learners respond, "Ones' place."

Have learners practice this activity by pointing to every digit, in each numeral below, and asking each time, "What place is this?"

Write the following on the board:

593,842,765,104,982
620,784,394,135
593,267,041
496,583
11,111,111
33,333
6,000,000,000

Have learners practice the examples of Facility Exercises #69 (Workbook I) to the level of facility; **then move on.** Please note: this activity is **oral**.

Write on the board:

257, 428, 345, 942, 584

Point to the ones' place and have learners say, "Ones."

Point to the next place and have learners say, "Tens."

Point to the next place and have learners say, "Hundreds."

Point to the next place and have learners say, "Ones of thousands."

Point to the next place and have learners say, "Tens of thousands."

Point to the next place and have learners say, "Hundreds of thousands."

Continuing similarly, learners will say, "Ones of millions," "Tens of millions," "Hundreds of millions," "Ones of billions," "Tens of billions," "Hundreds of billions," "Ones of trillions," "Tens of trillions," and "Hundreds of trillions."

Be sure to have individual children learn to recite, as above, from one end of the number to the other.

Please note that the thousands', millions', billions', and trillions' places can also be read as the "one thousands'," "one millions'," "one billions'," and "one trillions'," places respectively.

Be sure to expose learners to both types of expressions for these places.

COMPARING WHOLE NUMBERS

Objective: The learners will tell which of any two numerals is larger or smaller and explain why.

The prerequisites for comparing any two whole numbers are these:

1. Skill in counting; and,
2. Awareness that, in the process of counting forward, the number which precedes the next is the smaller of the two.

A learner skilled in counting will know, for example, that seven million, nine hundred seventy-eight thousand, eight hundred ninety-seven (7,978,897) will precede eight million, one hundred one thousand, two hundred thirteen (8,101,213) since:

(a) 7,978,897 is "in the seven millions";
(b) 8,101,213 is "in the eight millions"; and,
(c) every "seven millions number" precedes any "eight millions number."

Again, we know that 6,784,896 precedes 6,785,001, since:

(a) 6,784,896 is in the "six million, seven hundred eighty-four thousands";
(b) 6,785,001 is in the "six million, seven hundred eighty-five thousands"; and,
(c) every "six million, seven hundred eighty-four thousands number" precedes any "six million, seven hundred eighty-five thousands number."

We also know that 6,784,869 precedes 6,784,879 since:

(a) 6,784,869 is in the "six million, seven hundred eighty-four thousand, eight hundred sixties";
(b) 6,784,879 is in the "six million, seven hundred eighty-four thousand, eight hundred seventies"; and,
(c) every "six million, seven hundred eighty-four thousand, eight hundred sixties number" precedes any "six million, seven hundred eighty-four thousand, eight hundred seventies number."

Finally, we know that 96,275 precedes 105,000 since any number in the ten-thousands precedes any number in the hundred-thousands.

Consequently,

7,978,897 is less than 8,101,213;
6,784,896 is less than 6,785,001;
6,784,869 is less than 6,784,879; and
96,275 is less than 105,000.

Have learners answer the questions below.

"The number 8,530,465 is in which millions?" (In the eight millions)
"The number 8,530,465 is in which hundred-thousands?" (In the eight million, five hundred thousands)
"The number 8,530,465 is in which ten-thousands?" (In the eight million, five hundred thirty thousands)
"The number 8,530,465 is in which thousands?" (In the eight million, five hundred "thirty-zero" thousands)
"The number 8,530,465 is in which hundreds?" (In the eight million, five hundred thirty thousand, four hundreds)
"The number 8,530,465 is in which tens?" (In the eight million, five hundred thirty thousand, four hundred sixties)
"The number 8,530,465 is how many ones?" (Eight million, five hundred thirty thousand, four hundred sixty-five ones)

"The number 2,008,006 is in which millions?" (In the two millions)
"The number 2,008,006 is in which hundred-thousands?" (In the two million, zero hundred-thousands)
"The number 2,008,006 is in which ten-thousands?" (In the two million, zero ten-thousands)
"The number 2,008,006 is in which thousands?" (In the two million, eight thousands)
"The number 2,008,006 is in which hundreds?" (In the two million, eight thousand, zero hundreds)
"The number 2,008,006 is in which tens?" (In the two million, eight thousand, zero tens)
"The number 2,008,006 is how many ones?" (Two million, eight thousand, six ones)

Have learners practice the examples of Facility Exercises #70 (Workbook I) to the level of facility; **then move on.** Please note: this activity is **oral**.

The questions of Facility Exercises #70 will facilitate comparison of large whole numbers.

Consider, for example, which is larger: 8,530,465 or 8,531,000?

The comparison can be made as follows:

"Both numbers are in the eight millions. Does this tell us which is larger?"

"Both numbers are in the eight million, five hundred-thousands. Does this tell us which is larger?"

"Both numbers are in the eight million, five hundred thirty thousands. Does this tell us which is larger?"

"But one number is in the eight million, five hundred **thirty-zero thousands**, while the other is in the eight million, five hundred **thirty-one thousands**. Does this tell us which is larger?" (This tells us that 8,531,000 is larger than 8,530,465.)

Have learners practice the examples of Facility Exercises #71 (Workbook I) to the level of facility; **then move on.** Please note: this activity is **oral**.

FOR THE APPRECIATION OF THE METHOD FOR SUBTRACTING ONE LARGE NUMBER FROM ANOTHER

Objective: Learners will ask you to teach them the method for subtracting one large number from another.

Write on the board:

$$\begin{array}{r} 5 \\ -\underline{2} \end{array}$$

Have learners arrive at the answer to the above example by gathering a set of five objects, removing two of them, and counting the remaining number of objects.

Write on the board:

$$\begin{array}{r} 9 \\ -\underline{4} \end{array}$$

Have learners arrive at the answer to the above example by gathering a set of nine objects, removing four of them, and counting the remaining number of objects.

Write on the board:

$$\begin{array}{r} 19 \\ -\underline{12} \end{array}$$

Have learners arrive at the answer to the above example by gathering a set of nineteen objects, removing twelve of them, and counting the remaining number of objects.

Write on the board:

$$\begin{array}{r} 53 \\ -\underline{26} \end{array}$$

Have learners arrive at the answer to the above example by gathering a set of fifty-three objects, removing twenty-six of them, and counting the remaining number of objects.

Write on the board:

$$\begin{array}{r} 9{,}876 \\ -\ \underline{2{,}435} \end{array}$$

Try not to laugh, or even smile as you request that learners find the answer to the problem on the board by the same method used for the preceding examples.

Remain silent for a while and listen carefully to the expressions of their concerns and complaints.

You might facilitate the articulation of their concerns by asking such questions as, "Why don't you do this problem in the same way you did the others?" and, "How long do you think it would take to find the answer?"

Ask the learners, "Would you want to take a very 'lo-o-ong' time to finish this problem, or would you like to learn a short-cut which would take less than one minute?"

Tell the learners that the short-cut for subtracting one large number from another is called the subtraction algorithm.

Emphasize that the subtraction algorithm is a short-cut.

Now ask, "Do you want to learn the subtraction algorithm?" (All learners say, "YES!")

Tell learners they will be using the subtraction algorithm to subtract one large number from another (like the one on the board) in the near future.

SUBTRACTING ONE LARGE WHOLE NUMBER FROM ANOTHER
(without exchanging)

Objectives: The learners will

(a) subtract a whole number from a larger whole number where no regrouping is involved (the numerals may go up to the billions).

(b) respond, quickly and accurately, to questions involving the lower subtraction facts.

In this section, we will give learners intensive practice on subtraction examples (no regrouping) with numbers which go up to the billions.

By doing many of these, learners will continue to strengthen their power to instantly and accurately recall the lower subtraction facts.

The use of long subtractions as a vehicle for strengthening **quick mental recall of subtraction facts** permits learners to acquire both skills simultaneously.

At this point, we will not have the learners involved with place value as they do subtractions.

It is sufficient, for now, that they concentrate on acquiring the skill of subtracting one large number from another without regrouping.

After they have done an example, you must ask learners to read the top numeral, the bottom numeral, and the answer.

This provides some involvement with place value. You have seen earlier that the ability to read large numerals is related to the determination of place value.

Write the following on the board:

$$\begin{array}{r} 849{,}258{,}762{,}946 \\ -\ \underline{15{,}235{,}421{,}443} \end{array}$$

Have learners copy this example.

Be sure they take great pains to place the bottom digits "right under" corresponding digits in the top numeral.

Tell learners, "When I touch it, you say it."

Starting on the right, touch the 6.

Learners say, "Six."

Touch the minus sign.

Learners say, "Take away."

Touch the 3.

Learners say, "Three."

Ask, "What is six take away three?"

Tell learners, "Write the three right under the three."

Touch the top 4 in the next column.

Learners say, "Four."

Touch the minus sign.

Learners say, "Take away."

Touch the bottom 4.

Learners say, "Four."

Ask, "What is four take away four?"

Tell learners, "Write the zero right under the 4."

Continue similarly up to the ten billions' column.

Now touch the digit 8 in the last column.

Learners say, "Eight."

Touch the minus sign.

Learners say, "Take away."

Touch the blank space beneath the 8.

Have learners say, "Nothing."

Ask, "What is eight take away nothing?"

Tell learners, "Write the eight right under the eight."

Be sure to have learners "bring down" the commas and place them properly in the answer.

Have many learners make the following statement concerning the subtraction just completed:

> "Eight hundred forty-nine billion, two hundred fifty-eight million, seven hundred sixty-two thousand, nine hundred forty-six minus fifteen billion, two hundred thirty-five million, four hundred twenty-one thousand, four hundred forty-three equals eight hundred thirty-four billion, twenty-three million, three hundred forty-one thousand, five hundred three."

Have learners copy each example below and elicit responses as done above.

After each example is completed, have learners read the result (as in the above example) and check it.

(a)
$$\begin{array}{r} 697,483,857,697 \\ -\ \underline{302,462,534,342} \end{array}$$

(b)
$$\begin{array}{r} 67,248,648,953 \\ -\ \underline{\quad 214,423,521} \end{array}$$

(c)
$$\begin{array}{r} 84,856,789 \\ -\ \underline{82,253,153} \end{array}$$

For example, the checking of problem (a) above should be done as follows:

Learner's Work

Example (a)	Check
697,483,857,697	302,462,534,342
- 302,462,534,342	+ 395,021,323,355
395,021,323,355	697,483,857,697

Have learners practice the examples of Facility Exercises #72 (Workbook I) to the level of facility; **then move on.**

Facility Exercises #73 through #76 (Workbook I) provide mixed practice for the learners.

EQUIVALENT NUMERALS

Objectives: The learners will
(a) find many different names for a given numeral.
(b) explain the transformation of a sum to an equivalent sum.

Ask learners to hold up "six plus two fingers."

Now have a learner match the six plus two fingers in a one-to-one correspondence with the four plus four fingers of a partner (by actually touching fingers one to one).

Ask the questions:
"Which is greater: six plus two or four plus four?" (Neither is greater, since they match one to one)
"Are 6+2 and 4+4 the same number of fingers?"

Tell learners, "Since both 6+2 and 4+4 represent the same number, we say they are equal."

Write the following on the board:

6+2 = 4+4

Discuss as follows:
"The expression 6+2 is the name of a number; so is 4+4."
"Is 6+2 the same name as 4+4?" (No)
"The equal sign between 6+2 and 4+4 tells us that they are the same number."
"The numerals 6+2 and 4+4 are different names for the same number."

Hold up eight fingers and say,
"'Six plus two' is a name for this many fingers."
"'Four plus four' is also a name for this many fingers."
"What is another name for this many fingers?"

"This many" still refers to the eight extended fingers.

Learners may offer the following names for the number of fingers which are extended: "eight"; "seven plus one"; "one plus seven"; "two plus six"; "five plus three"; "three plus three plus two"; and so on.

You may point out that all the above names (for the number of extended fingers) involve the plus sign.

With the same number of fingers extended, ask, "Can you give me a name for this many fingers which has a minus sign?"

Give learners examples of other names for the number of extended fingers such as: "Ten minus two"; "Nine minus one"; "Three plus three plus three minus one"; and so on.

Here is a list of all the above names for the number of extended fingers:

6+2, 4+4, 8, 7+1, 1+7, 2+6
5+3, 3+3+2, 10–2, 9–1, 3+3+3–1

Tell learners that since we have **eleven different names for the same number**, we can write the following on the board:

6+2 = 4+4 = 8 = 7+1 = 1+7 = 2+6 = 5+3 = 3+3+2 = 10–2 = 9–1 = 3+3+3–1

Write the following pairs of numerals on the board:

3+2, 8–1	5+5, 7–1	6–2, 3+1	3+3+3, 4+4+1
3+3, 6	5, 2+4	10–3, 4+3	8–5, 7–4

Ask the following questions:
"Are the numerals 3+2 and 8–1 different names for the same number?"
"Are the numerals 6-2 and 3+1 different names for the same number?"
"Are the numerals 3+3 and 6 different names for the same number?"

Ask the same question about the remaining pairs of numerals.

Tell learners that one number may have different names, just as one person may have different names.

Ask some learners, "How many different names do you have?"

Write the following on the board:

7+3=5+4 2+2=10–6 3+3=2+2+2 1+1=7–6 4+4=2+2+2+2
8–3=2+1+2 5–5=9–9 1=1+0 5+5=3+3+3 9–4=10–5 5–3=9–6

Ask the following questions:
"Is 7+3 = 5+4?"
"Is 2+2 = 10–6?"
"Is 3+3 = 2+2+2?"

Ask the same question about the remaining equations above.

Have learners practice the examples of Facility Exercises #77 (Workbook I) to the level of facility; **then move on.**

Place a set of three blocks (or other available objects) separate from, but close to, a set of six blocks.

A name for the total number of blocks is 3+6.

Have a learner take one block from the set of three and place it with the set of six.

Ask the following questions:

"Has the total number of blocks changed?"

"What new name do you get for the total number of blocks, by simply looking at the two sets?" (2+7)

Have a learner take one block from the set of two, and place it with the set of seven.

Ask the following questions:

"Has the total number of blocks changed?"

"What new name do you get for the total number of blocks, by simply looking at the two sets?" (1+8)

Have a learner take three blocks from the set of eight, and place them with the set of one.

Ask the following questions:

"Has the total number of blocks changed?"

"What new name do you get for the total number of blocks, by simply looking at the two sets?" (4+5)

"Are 3+6, 2+7, 1+8, and 4+5 different names for the same number?"

Write the following on the board:

$$3 + 6 = 2 + 7 = 1 + 8 = 4 + 5$$

Tell learners that since the above numerals are different names for the same number,we can put equal signs between them.

Place a set of two blocks close to a set of eight blocks.

Ask, "What name do you get for the total number of blocks, by simply looking at the two sets?" (2+8)

Have a learner take four blocks from the set of eight, and place them with the set of two.

Ask the following questions:

"Has the total number of blocks changed?"

"What new name do you get for the total number of blocks, by simply looking at the two sets?" (6+4)

Have a learner take three blocks from the set of six, and place them with the set of four.

Ask the following questions:
"Has the total number of blocks changed?"
"What new name do you get for the total number of blocks, by simply looking at the two sets?" (3+7)

Have a learner take six blocks from the set of seven, and place them with the set of three.

Ask the following questions:
"Has the total number of blocks changed?"
"What new name do you get for the total number of blocks, by simply looking at the two sets?" (9+1)
"Are 2+8, 6+4, 3+7, and 9+1 different names for the same number?"

Write the following on the board:

$$2 + 8 = 6 + 4 = 3 + 7 = 9 + 1$$

Remind learners that the equal signs say these four numerals (2+8, 6+4, 3+7, 9+1) are different names for the same number.

We will now find different names for the same number without the use of blocks (or other concrete materials).

We know that 6+2 is the name of a certain number.

Remember that 8 is also a **name** for that number and is not the number itself.

Direct learners as follows:
"Look at the 6 in 6+2 and take 3 from it. What's left?" (3)
"Add that 3 to the 2 in 6+2. What do you get?" (5)
"So if we take 3 from the 6 and give it to the 2, what new name for the number 6+2 do we have?" (3+5)
"Look at the 3 in 3+5 and take 2 from it. What's left?" (1)
"Add that 2 to the 5 in 3+5. What do you get?" (7)
"So if we take 2 from the 3 and give it to the 5, what new name for the number 3+5 do we have?" (1+7)
"Look at the 7 in 1+7 and take 6 from it. What's left?" (1)
"Add that 6 to the 1 in 1+7. What do you get?" (7)
"So if we take 6 from the 7 and give it to the 1, what new name for the number 1+7 do we have?" (7+1)
"Do you see that 6+2, 3+5, 1+7, and 7+1 are different names for the same number?"

"Are 1+7 and 7+1 different names?"
"Do 1+7 and 7+1 look different? Do they sound different when you say them?" (They are different)

Repeat the above sufficiently often for learners to understand that subtracting from one number, and adding (the same) to the other, does not change the sum.

Note that the learners can know 2+8 and 6+4 are equal by seeing that they are both equal to 10.

It is very important for learners to function in this manner.

However, for the sake of transforming "nine-plus" addition facts into equivalent "ten-plus" addition facts (which occurs a few pages hence), learners must be aware that 2+8 and 6+4 are equal simply because we subtract 4 from 8 and add it to the 2.

Facility with this kind of transformation is the means by which learners will quickly know the nine-plus, eight-plus, seven-plus, and six-plus addition facts (examples of these types of facts are 9+5, 8+3, 7+5, and 6+6 respectively) **without memorization**.

Below is an example of a typical question in Facility Exercises #78 and the expected answer.

Question: How can we transform 3+6 into 7+2?

Answer: By taking 4 from the 6 and adding it to the 3.

Have learners practice the examples in Facility Exercises #78 (Workbook I) to the level of facility; **then move on.** Please note: this activity is **oral**.

THE TEN-PLUS ADDITION FACTS

Objective: The learners will quickly tell the sum of ten and any number from one to nine inclusive.

Write the following on the board:

```
10  +  7
 \     |
teen  seven
```

Remind the learners that another name for ten is "teen."

Tell learners, "Say it when I touch it."

Touch the 7. Learners say, "Seven."

Touch the 10. Learners say, "Teen."

Ask,
"So ten plus seven equals _____?" (Seventeen)
"What are seven plus ten?"

Repeat the above activity for 10+6, 6+10, 10+8, 8+10, 10+4, 4+10, 10+9, 9+10.

Inform learners of the following:
"Fifteen is the answer for 10+5; not 'fiveteen.'"
"Thirteen is the answer for 10+3; not 'threeteen.'"
"Twelve is the answer for 10+2; not 'twoteen.'"
"Eleven is the answer for 10+1; not 'oneteen.'"

Have learners practice the ten-plus addition facts to facility on the oral level.

Have learners practice the examples of Facility Exercises #79 (Workbook I) to the level of facility; **then move on.**

MASTERING THE HIGHER ADDITION FACTS WITHOUT MEMORIZATION

Objective: The learners will rapidly and accurately provide answers to the higher addition facts. No memorization is involved.

In order to prepare learners for the "9+," "8+," "7+," and "6+" addition facts, it is necessary to review the earlier exercises which linked 9 and 1, 8 and 2, 7 and 3, 6 and 4.

Write the following on the board:

9 + 8

Point to the 9 and ask, "Is this teen?"

Ask the following questions:
"How much does 9 need to become teen?" (Learners will say, "One more," since 9 and 1 are linked in their minds)
"Where will 9 get the 1 from?" (From the 8)

Tell learners, "Hold up 8 fingers and 'throw one' to the nine." (Learners will throw 1 to the 9 by folding one of the 8 extended fingers)

Explain that the 1 thrown "goes over" to the 9 to make the teen.

The seven fingers left, plus the teen, make seventeen; so 9+8 equals seventeen.

Tell learners that after throwing one finger, they only have to look at their hands, and they will know the answer (seven fingers left trigger "seventeen").

Write the following on the board:

9 + 5

Ask the following questions:
"How much does 9 need to become teen?"
"Where will 9 get the 1 from?"

Tell learners,

"Hold up 5 fingers and throw 1 to the 9. Now look at your hand and you'll know the answer." (Four fingers left trigger "fourteen")

"So 9+5 equals 14."

Similarly have learners demonstrate the following:

9 + 9 = 18	9 + 4 = 13	9 + 7 = 16
9 + 6 = 15	9 + 2 = 11	9 + 3 = 12

Note: Please **do not** spend even one day practicing 9+ only. This is a mistake since learners may acquire a fixation on throwing one finger, in spite of the fact that 8+, 7+, and 6+ require the throwing of two fingers, three fingers, and four fingers respectively.

Write the following on the board:

8 + 7

Ask the following questions:

"How much does 8 need to become teen?" (Learners will say, "Two more," since 8 and 2 are linked in their minds)

"Where will 8 get the 2 from?"

Tell learners,

"Hold up 7 fingers and throw 2 to the 8. Now look at your hand and you'll know the answer." (The 2 fingers "go over" to 8 to make the teen and the 5 fingers left trigger "fifteen")

"So 8 + 7 equals 15."

Similarly have learners demonstrate the following:

8 + 8 = 16	8 + 4 = 12
8 + 6 = 14	8 + 3 = 11
8 + 5 = 13	

Write the following on the board:

7 + 7

Ask the following questions:

"How much does 7 need to become teen?" (Learners will say, "Three more," since 7 and 3 are linked in their minds)

"Where will 7 get the 3 from?"

Tell learners,

"Hold up 7 fingers and throw 3 to the other 7. Now look at your hand, and you'll know the answer." (Four fingers left trigger "fourteen")

"So 7 + 7 equals 14."

Similarly have learners demonstrate the following:

7 + 6 = 13	7 + 5 = 12	7 + 4 = 11

By throwing 4 fingers to 6, have learners demonstrate the following:

6 + 6 = 12   6 + 5 = 11

From this point onward, it is important to give **mixed oral practice.**

This means that in any one lesson, questions asked should involve a mixture of 10+, 9+, 8+, 7+, and 6+.

Note that it is more useful to think of 6+9, for instance, as a 9+ example rather than a 6+; since it is easier to throw 1 to 9 than 4 to 6.

The following are 9+ examples:

9 + 9, 9 + 8, 8 + 9, 9 + 7, 7 + 9
9 + 6, 6 + 9, 9 + 5, 5 + 9, 9 + 4
4 + 9, 9 + 3, 3 + 9, 9 + 2, 2 + 9

The following are 8+ examples:

8 + 8, 8 + 7, 7 + 8, 8 + 6, 6 + 8, 8 + 5
5 + 8, 8 + 4, 4 + 8, 8 + 3, 3 + 8

The following are 7+ examples:

7 + 7, 7 + 6, 6 + 7, 7 + 5, 5 + 7, 7 + 4, 4 + 7

The following are 6+ examples:

6 + 6, 6 + 5, 5 + 6

The **Professor B Math Chart #5** is used by many teachers to play an exciting, rapid-response game called "Snatch."

This game encourages learners to cognitively process the strategies of this section, as quickly as possible, in order to arrive at the answers to the higher addition facts **without fingers**.

The **Professor B Math Chart #6** is used for daily practice toward permanent and instant recall of these facts.

Have learners practice (to the level of facility) the use of fingers (as described above) to find answers to the higher addition facts (sum between 10 and 19).

After they have acquired facility with fingers, you should have them learn to "throw" the numbers in their minds, and tell you the answers.

This may happen slowly at first but will speed up with practice.

After much practice on these cognitive strategies for knowing the higher addition facts, provide more by means of the examples in Facility Exercises #80 and #81 (Workbook I). Practice to the level of facility: **then move on.**

ADDING ANY TWO WHOLE NUMBERS
(with regrouping)

Objectives: The learners will

(a) add any two whole numbers up to the millions with regrouping; and

(b) respond, quickly and accurately, to questions involving addition facts with sum greater than ten and less than nineteen.

In this section, we will give learners intensive practice in addition (with regrouping) involving large numbers. Assigning many of these long additions to learners permits them to make intensive use of the nine-plus, eight-plus, seven-plus, six-plus, and other addition facts. They will achieve quick recall of these facts in the same way that you remember phone numbers which you use frequently. The use of **long additions with regrouping** as a vehicle for attaining **quick recall of these facts** permits learners to acquire both skills simultaneously.

At this point, we will not have learners involved with place value as they do addition examples. It is sufficient, for now, that they concentrate on acquiring the skill of adding large numbers with regrouping. After completing an addition, ask a learner to read the top numeral, the bottom numeral, and the answer.

Write the following on the board:

$$\begin{array}{r} 2{,}847{,}936 \\ +\ \underline{5{,}825{,}948} \end{array}$$

Have learners copy this addition.

Tell learners, "Say what I touch."

Starting on the right, touch the 6 (learners say, "Six"); touch the plus sign (learners say, "Plus"); and touch the 8 (learners say, "Eight").

Ask the following questions:
"What are 6 plus 8?"
"When you say, 'fourteen,' do you hear four and teen?"

Tell learners to place the 4 right under the 8, and write the 1, representing teen, above "the next door neighbor" which is 3.

If learners do not recall the answer to 6+8, elicit the result as follows:
"Hold up the smaller number on your fingers."
"How much will you throw to the 8?"
"Throw it."
"So 6+8 equals ______?"

Tell learners, "Say what I touch."

In the second column from the right, touch the 3 (learners say, "Three"); touch the plus sign (learners say, "Plus"); and touch the 4 (learners say, "Four").

Ask, "What are 3 plus 4?"

Tell learners to add the 1 (above the 3) to the 7.

Ask the following questions:
"Where do you write the 8?" (Have learners write the 8 under the 4)
"Is there a 'teen' to take to the next door neighbor?" (No. We got 8; not 18)

Tell learners, "Say what I touch."

In the third column from the right, touch the top 9 (learners say, "Nine"); touch the plus sign (learners say, "Plus"); and touch the bottom 9 (learners say, "Nine").

Ask the following questions:
"What are 9 plus 9?"
"When you say, 'Eighteen,' do you hear eight and teen?"
"Where will you write the 8?" (Under the 9)
"Where does the 1, representing teen, go?" (On top of the next door neighbor, 7)

Have learners place the 8 under the 9, and write the 1 on top of the 7.

If learners do not recall the answer to 9+9, elicit the result as follows:
"Hold up 9 fingers."
"How much will you throw to the other nine?"
"Throw it."
"So 9+9 equals ______?"

Tell learners, "Say what I touch."

In the fourth column from the right, touch the 7, the plus sign, and the 5.

Learners say, "Seven plus 5."

Ask the following questions:
"What are 7 plus 5?"
"Do you see anything more to add in this column?"

Tell learners, "Don't forget to add the 1 above the 7."

Ask, "When you say, 'Thirteen,' do you hear three and teen?"

Tell learners, "Write the 3 and the 1 where you think they should go." (The 3 goes under the 5 and the 1 goes above the next door neighbor, 4)

If learners do not recall the answer to 7+5, elicit as follows:
"Hold up the smaller number on your fingers."
"How much will you throw to the 7?"
"Throw it."
"So 7+5 equals _____?"

Tell learners, "Say what I touch."

In the fifth column from the right, touch the 4, the plus sign, and the 2.

Learners say, "Four plus 2."

Ask the following questions:
"What are 4 plus 2?"
"Do you see anything more to add in this column?"

Tell learners,
"Don't forget to add the 1 above the 4."
"Write the 7 where you think it should go."

Ask, "Is there a teen to go above the next door neighbor?" (No)

Tell learners, "Say what I touch."

In the sixth column from the right, touch the 8, the plus sign, and the bottom 8.

Learners say, "Eight plus 8."

Ask the following questions:
"What are 8 plus 8?"
"Do you see anything more to add in this column?"
"When you say, 'Sixteen,' do you hear six and teen?"

Tell learners, "Write the 6 and the 1 where you think they should go."

If learners do not recall 8+8, elicit by means of fingers.

Tell learners, "Say what I touch."

In the last column, touch the 2, the plus sign, and the 5.

Learners say, "Two plus 5."

Ask the following questions:
"What are 2 plus 5?"
"Do you see anything more to add in this column?"
"So what do you write under the 5?" (8)

Learners must place the commas properly in the answer.

Have many learners make the following statement concerning the addition just completed:

"Two million, eight hundred forty-seven thousand, nine hundred thirty-six plus five million, eight hundred twenty-five thousand, nine hundred forty-eight equals eight million, six hundred seventy-three thousand, eight hundred eighty-four."

Lead learners through the following addition examples in the same manner as above.

(a)	1,582,963 + 2,863,574	(c)	9,263,158 + 6,043,064
(b)	4,723,606 + 3,752,876		4,652,831 + 9,652,831

Note that in example (c), the last column (9+6) adds up to 15.

Tell learners that since there is no next door neighbor (on the left), the teen must be written next to the 5.

Our objective, at this point, is to have learners develop the capacity to do these long additions by themselves, with a minimum of mistakes.

As you know, it is possible for an expert adult "arithmetician" to get the wrong answer occasionally.

Of greatest importance, therefore, is that learners:

(a) have the "know-how" (as does the expert); and

(b) are provided with **sufficient and continuous practice** as a means of minimizing errors.

It must be understood that getting the wrong answer does not necessarily mean "it's too difficult for them."

In fact, once we have diagnosed (through observation of the learners at work) that they have the know-how, an excessive number of wrong answers (in a set of long additions) merely provides objective feedback, which informs us that more practice is necessary.

The introduction of learners to long additions (with regrouping) must be done with great care.

Do not, at this point, give learners an example and tell them to do it by themselves.

Proceed as follows:

1. Write an example on the board (similar to those above) and have learners

copy it.
2. Tell them to add the **first** column on the right by themselves.
3. Walk around the room and check the learners' work. Ascertain the types of errors they tend to make.
4. Do the first column on the board while commenting on their errors.
5. Tell them to add the second column by themselves.
6. Repeat Step #3.
7. Do the second column on the board, while commenting on their errors.
8. Continue similarly doing **one column** at a time.

Follow this "one-column-at-a-time" procedure **on a daily basis,** until learners have facility with it.

Now proceed as follows:

1. Write an example on the board and have learners copy it.
2. Tell them to add the **first two** columns by themselves.
3. Walk around the room and check the learners' work. Ascertain the types of errors they tend to make.
4. Do the two columns on the board while commenting on their errors.
5. Tell them to add the next two columns by themselves.
6. Repeat Step #3 and Step #4.
7. Continue doing two columns at a time, followed by steps 3 and 4.

Follow the "two-columns-at-a-time" procedure **on a daily basis,** until learners have facility with it.

Repeat the above activity for "three-columns-at-a-time," then "four-columns-at-a-time"; and so on.

You can now have learners do whole long addition examples by themselves.

You may wonder how much time should be spent on two-columns-at-a-time, or three-columns-at-a-time, and so on.

The answer is simply to wait until mistakes (with the number of columns being worked on) begin to occur infrequently.

Playing "Snatch" with the use of the Professor B Math Chart #5 and follow-up activity with Professor B Math Chart #6 will significantly reduce the amount of time spent on the activity of this section, since learners will quickly acquire instant recall of the higher addition facts.

Have learners practice the examples of Facility Exercises #82 (Workbook I) to the level of facility; **then move on**.

The next set of exercises is provided for **independent work** by the learners.

Have learners practice the examples of Facility Exercises #83 (Workbook I) to the level of facility; **then move on**.

PREPARING FOR SUBTRACTION WITH EXCHANGING

Objective: The learners will tell whether we can take a one-digit number from another one-digit number.

Have learners see you place four blocks in a bag.

Ask the following questions:
"Can you take one block out of this bag?"
"How many will be left?" (3)
"Can you take two blocks out of this bag?"
"How many will be left?"
"Can you take three blocks out of this bag?"
"How many will be left?"
"Can you take four blocks out of this bag?"
"How many will be left?"
"Can you take five blocks out of this bag?"
"Can you take six blocks out of this bag?"

Have learners see you place five blocks in a bag.

Ask the following questions:
"Can you take 3 blocks from 5?"
"Can you take 1 block from 5?"
"Can you take 6 blocks from 5?"
"Can you take 8 blocks from 5?"
"Can you take 2 blocks from 5?"
"Can you take 5 blocks from 5?"
"Can you take 7 blocks from 5?"
"Can you take 9 blocks from 5?"
"Can you take 4 blocks from 5?"

Have learners practice the examples of Facility Exercises #84 (Workbook I) to the level of facility; **then move on**. Please note: this activity is **oral**.

MASTERING THE HIGHER SUBTRACTION FACTS WITHOUT MEMORIZATION

Objective: The learners will rapidly and accurately provide answers to the higher subtraction facts.

$11 - 2$

$11 - 3 \quad 12 - 3$

$11 - 4 \quad 12 - 4 \quad 13 - 4$

$11 - 5 \quad 12 - 5 \quad 13 - 5 \quad 14 - 5$

$11 - 6 \quad 12 - 6 \quad 13 - 6 \quad 14 - 6 \quad 15 - 6$

$11 - 7 \quad 12 - 7 \quad 13 - 7 \quad 14 - 7 \quad 15 - 7 \quad 16 - 7$

$11 - 8 \quad 12 - 8 \quad 13 - 8 \quad 14 - 8 \quad 15 - 8 \quad 16 - 8 \quad 17 - 8$

$11 - 9 \quad 12 - 9 \quad 13 - 9 \quad 14 - 9 \quad 15 - 9 \quad 16 - 9 \quad 17 - 9 \quad 18 - 9$

In this section, learners will learn to think rapidly through any one of the above subtraction facts.

Learners will acquire immediate recall of these facts when using them intensively.

In the set of subtractions above, we will begin with an example from the second row (from the bottom).

Write the following on the board:

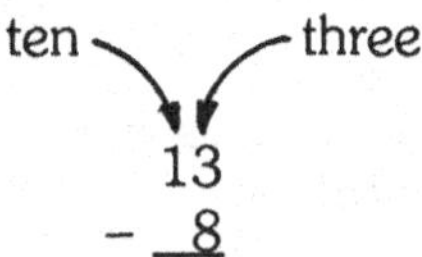

Now do the following:

Point to the 3 (in the 13 above) and ask, "What does this represent?"
Point to the 1 (in the 13 above) and ask, "What does this represent?" (Ten)
Point to the 3 again and say, "Show me this many fingers."
Point to the 1 again and say, "Show me this many fingers." (Be sure they show all ten fingers)

Now tell them to pretend they are placing the 3 in one pocket, and the 10 in the other.

The example asks them to "take away" 8 from 13.

Ask the following questions:

"Can we take the 8 out of the 'three pocket'?" (No)
"If we can't take 8 out of the three pocket, where will we take it from?" (The "ten pocket")
"Take the 8 out of your 10 pocket. What's left in your ten pocket?" (2)
"And what's left in your other pocket?" (3)
"What's left altogether?" (5)
"So 13 take away 8 equals ______?" (5)
"And what is 5 + 8?" (13)

Note: The teacher is strongly advised to go through many of the examples above by actively involving the learners in "pocket subtraction."

After learners have acquired facility in pocket subtraction, you may modify the dialogue as follows below.

Write the following on the board:

$$\begin{array}{r} 15 \\ -\underline{6} \end{array}$$

Ask the following questions:

"Can we take the 6 out of the 5?"
"So what will we take the 6 from?"
"Take the 6 from the 10. What's left?" (4)
"Did we take anything from the 5?"
"So what's left in the ones' place?" (5)
"What's left altogether?" (4+5=9)
"So 15 take away 6 equals ______?"

After leading the learners through many of these subtractions by means of the second approach, have them move on to the next strategy which is more concise.

Below you will see a two-step description of a strategy for speeding up the learners' cognitive processing of these subtraction facts.

Step #1

Write the following on the board:

(1)	(2)	(3)	(4)	(5)	(6)	(7)
12	12	12	12	12	12	12
– 3	– 4	– 5	– 6	– 7	– 8	– 9

Ask the learners, "Do you remember the game we played with ten? When I said nine, you said one. When I said three, you said seven. When I said eight, what did you say?"

Learners respond, "Two."

If necessary, return to this game and review it.

Now take your pointer and touch the 7 (in Example #5) on the board.

Tell the learners that when you touch 7, they must say, "Three" instantly.

Touch 3 (in Example #l) on the board.

Learners respond, "Seven."

Touch 9 (in Example #7).

Learners respond, "One."

Similarly, touch the other numbers (the subtrahends) in the other examples on the board.

Be sure learners are responding rapidly and correctly.

Step #2

Select Example #2 on the board.

Tell the learners that when you touch 4, they must say, "Six," but as you move the pointer up (to the minuend) and touch 2, they must continue to say, "____ plus two, eight."

In other words, you touch the 4 and then the 2.

Learners respond, "Six plus two, eight."

You must immediately conclude: "So twelve minus four equals eight."

Select Example #6 on the board.

Touch the 8 and then the 2.

Learners respond, "Two plus two, four."

You must immediately conclude: "So twelve minus eight equals four."

Select Example #3 on the board.

Touch the 5 and then the 2.

Learners respond, "Five plus two, seven."

You must immediately conclude: "So twelve minus five equals seven."

All the subtraction examples in the triangular arrangement above, can be cognitively processed in this manner.

Write the following examples on the board:

(1)	(2)	(3)
16	11	15
- 9	- 3	- 6

In a manner similar to the pattern previously established,

1. touch 9, then 6 (Example #1), and have the learners respond, "One plus six, seven; so sixteen minus nine equals seven."
2. touch 3, then 1 (Example #2), and have the learners respond, "Seven plus one, eight; so eleven minus three equals eight."
3. touch 6, then 5 (Example #3), and have the learners respond, "Four plus five, nine; so fifteen minus six equals nine."

The Professor B Math Chart #7 is used by many teachers to play an exciting, rapid-response game.

This game encourages learners to cognitively process the strategies of Step #2, as quickly as possible, in order to arrive at the answers to the higher subtraction facts without fingers.

Using the Step #2 technique, have learners practice the examples of Facility Exercises #85 (Workbook I) to the level of facility; **then move on**.

SUBTRACTING ONE WHOLE NUMBER FROM ANOTHER (with exchanging)

Objectives: The learners will

(a) subtract a whole number from a larger whole number where regrouping is involved. The numbers may go up to the millions.

(b) respond, quickly and accurately, to questions involving the higher subtraction facts.

In this section, we will give the learners intensive practice on subtraction (with regrouping) involving large numbers. Assigning many of these long subtractions to learners, permits them to make intensive use of the subtraction facts in the previous section. They will achieve quick recall of these facts in the same way that you remember the phone numbers which you use frequently. The use of **long subtractions** as a vehicle for attaining **quick recall** of these facts, permits learners to acquire both skills simultaneously.

At this point, we will not have learners involved with place value, as they do subtraction examples. It is sufficient, for now, that they concentrate on acquiring the skill of subtracting large numbers, with regrouping. After completing a subtraction, ask a learner to read the top numeral, the bottom numeral, and the answer.

Write the following on the board:

$$\begin{array}{r} 638{,}596{,}478 \\ -\ \underline{274{,}827{,}684} \end{array}$$

Have learners copy this example.

Tell them, "Say what I touch."

Starting on the right, touch the 8, the minus sign, and the 4. Learners say, "Eight take away 4."

Tell learners,

"Hold up the top number on your fingers."

"Look at your own 8 fingers."

Be sure learners look at their own 8 fingers.

Now ask the following questions:
"Can you take 4 away from 8?"
"Is 8 large enough to take away 4?"
"How much is left?" (Four)
"Where do we write the 4?"

Have learners write the 4 under the 4.

Tell them, "Say what I touch."

In the second column from the right, touch the 7, the minus sign, and the 8.

Learners say, "Seven take away 8."

Tell learners,
"Hold up the top number on your fingers."
"Look at your own 7 fingers."

Be sure learners look at their own 7 fingers. Now ask the following questions:
"Can you take 8 away from 7?"
"Is 7 large enough to take away 8?"

Tell learners,
"Since 7 is not large enough to take away 8, the 7 needs help."
"Seven says, 'Help!' to the next door neighbor."
"So, we go next door to the 4; cross it out; take 1 from it; write a small 3 above the 4; and write one next to the 7."

Ask the following questions:
"Now is 17 large enough to take away 8?"
"What is 17 take away 8?"
"Where do we write the 9?"

Have learners write the 9 under the 8.

If a learner does not recall "17–8," you might elicit the answer by pointing to the 17, asking,
"Will we take the 8 from the 7 or the teen?"
"Take the 8 from the teen. What's left?"
"Two plus 7 equals ______?"
"So 17 take away 8 equals ______?"

You might elicit the answer more quickly by having the learners say, "Two plus 7 equals 9; so 17 minus 8 equals 9."

Tell learners, "Say what I touch."

In the third column from the right, touch the 3 (above the 4), the minus sign and the 6.

Learners say, "Three take away 6."

Tell learners,
"Hold up the top number on your fingers."
"Look at your own 3 fingers."

Ask the following questions:
"Can you take 6 away from 3?"
"Is 3 large enough to take away 6?"
"Since 3 is not large enough to take away 6, what does 3 say to the next door neighbor?" (Help!)

Tell learners, "So, we go next door to the 6; cross it out; take 1 from it; write a small 5 above the 6; and write 1 next to the 3." Ask the following questions:
"Now is 13 large enough to take away 6?"
"What is 13 take away 6?"
"Where do we write the 7?"

Have learners write the 7 under the 6.

If a learner does not recall "13 – 6," you might elicit the answer by having him or her say, "Four plus 3 equals 7; so 13 minus 6 equals 7."

Tell learners, "Say what I touch."

In the fourth column from the right, touch the 5 (above the 6), the minus sign, and the 7.

Learners say, "Five take away 7."

Tell learners,
"Hold up the top number on your fingers."
"Look at your own 5 fingers."

Ask the following questions:
"Can you take 7 away from 5?"
"Is 5 large enough to take away 7?"
"What does 5 say to the next door neighbor?"

Have learners explain that they must go next door to the 9; cross it out; take 1 from it; write a small 8 above the 9; and write 1 next to the 5.

Ask the following questions:
"Now is 15 large enough to take away 7?"
"What is 15 take away 7?"
"Where do we write the 8?"

Have learners write the 8 under the 7.

If a learner does not recall "fifteen take away 7," you might elicit the answer by having him or her say, "Three plus 5 equals 8; so 15 minus 7 equals 8."

By means of similar dialogues, lead learners through the rest of the original subtraction example.

Be sure to have learners explain what they must do when they go over to the next door neighbor.

When completed, the example should appear as below:

```
 5  7    8 15 13
 638,596,478
-274,827,684
 363,768,794
```

Have many learners make the following statement concerning the subtraction just completed:

> "Six hundred thirty-eight million, five hundred ninety-six thousand, four hundred seventy-eight minus two hundred seventy-four million, eight hundred twenty-seven thousand, six hundred eighty-four equals three hundred sixty-three million, seven hundred sixty-eight thousand, seven hundred ninety-four."

Lead learners through the subtraction examples below in the same manner as above.

```
(a)    2,863,544        (c)    9,263,156
     - 1,582,973             - 6,043,064

(b)    5,723,606        (d)    5,243,715
     - 3,752,876             - 1,456,139
```

Our objective, at this point, is to have learners develop the capacity to do these long subtractions by themselves with a minimum of errors.

Remember that once the learner is diagnosed (through observation of his or her work) as having the "know-how," an excessive number of wrong answers merely provides objective feedback which informs us that more practice is necessary.

The introduction of learners to long subtraction (with regrouping) must be done with great care.

Do not (at this point) give learners an example and tell them to do it by themselves.

Proceed as follows:

1. Write an example on the board (in which regrouping is necessary more often than not) and have learners copy it.
2. Tell them to subtract in the **first** column by themselves.

3. Walk around the room and check the learners' work. Ascertain the types of errors they tend to make.
4. Do the first column on the board while commenting on their errors.
5. Tell them to subtract in the **second** column by themselves.
6. Repeat Step #3.
7. Do the second column on the board, while commenting on their errors.
8. Continue similarly doing **one column** at a time.

Follow this "one-column-at-a-time" procedure **on a daily basis,** until learners have facility with it.

Then follow the "two-columns-at-a-time" procedure **on a daily basis,** until learners have facility with it.

Repeat the above for "three-columns-at-a-time," then "four-columns-at-a-time"; and so on.

You can eventually have learners do whole long subtractions by themselves.

Playing the game associated with the Professor B Math Chart #7 will significantly reduce the amount of time spent on the activity of this section, since learners will acquire instant recall of the higher subtraction facts.

The examples in the facility exercises below are provided for carrying out the above procedures.

Have learners practice the examples of Facility Exercises #86 (Workbook I) to the level of facility; **then move on**.

The next set of exercises is provided for **independent work** by the learners.

Have them **check** each example.

Demonstrate to learners as follows:

Learner's Work

Example	**Check**
7,283	547
− 547	+ 6,736
6,736	7,283

Tell learners the subtraction is done correctly since the check shows that when the answer, 6,736, is added to 547, we "get back" the 7,283.

Have learners practice the examples of Facility Exercises #87 (Workbook I) to the level of facility; **then move on**.

Have learners copy the following example:

```
  7,000
- 2,537
```

Tell learners, "Say what I touch."

Starting on the right, touch the zero, the minus sign, and the 7. Learners say, "Zero take away 7."

Ask the following questions:
"Can you take 7 away from zero?"
"Is zero large enough to take away 7?"
"Can zero get help from the next door neighbor?"

Have learners see that we cannot take 1 from a next door neighbor which is zero.

Ask, "So where do we go for help?"

Have learners see that we must go over to the 7; cross it out and take 1 from it; write a small 6 above it; and write 1 next to the zero just to the right of 7.

Learners must do this on their own example. See below.

```
  6
  7̸,¹000
- 2,537
```

Tell learners, "Now we cross out the 10; take 1 from it; write a small 9 above it; and write 1 next to the middle zero."

Have learners do this on their own examples. See below.

```
  6 9
  7̸,1̸0̸¹00
- 2,537
```

Tell learners, "Again we cross out the 10; take 1 from it; write a small 9 above it; and write 1 next to the zero on the right."

Have learners do this on their own examples. See below.

```
  6 9 9
  7̸,1̸0̸1̸0̸¹0
- 2,537
```

Now lead learners through the example as follows:
"Ten take away 7 equals ______?"
"Nine take away 3 equals ______?"
"Nine take away 5 equals ______?"
"Six take away 2 equals ______?"

Have learners complete their own example.

Learners must say the following:

> "Seven thousand minus two thousand five hundred thirty-seven equals four thousand four hundred sixty-three."

Have learners **check** this example.

Write the following on the board:

```
   9,000
 - 2,387

  40,000
 -  8,907

 100,000
 - 45,763
```

Lead learners through the above subtractions.

Have learners check each of these examples.

Have them practice similar examples in Facility Exercises #88 (Workbook I) to the level of facility; **then move on**.

PLACE VALUE RELATIONSHIPS

Objectives: The learners will state that

(a) ten of a unit belonging to a particular place in a numeral representing a whole number equal one unit belonging one place to its left.

(b) one of a unit belonging to a particular place in a numeral representing a whole number equals ten units belonging one place to its right.

Write the following on the board:

123,456,789,123,456

Ten ______ equal one ______.

Tell learners, "Ten of any unit in one place of a whole number equals one unit in the place to its left."

Draw arrows on the board pointing to the digits 5 and 6 at the right side of the number above.

Take your pointer, touch the 6 and ask, "What place is this?"

Learners respond, "Ones'."

Touch the 5 and ask, "What place is this?"

Learners respond, "Tens'."

Now have the learners focus on the statement on the board (with the blank spaces).

Tell them to place the word "ones" in the first blank space (on the left) and "ten" in the second.

The statement is now read as follows by the learners: "Ten ones equal one ten."

This is the interpretation of the statement below the number (on the board) as applied to the places indicated by the arrows.

Erase the arrow pointing to the digit 6 and draw arrows pointing to the digits 5 and 4 (on the right side of the number).

Take your pointer, touch the 5 and ask, "What place is this?"

Learners respond, "Tens'."

Touch the 4 and ask, "What place is this?"

Learners respond, "Hundreds'."

Have learners focus on the statement on the board (with the blank spaces).

Tell them to place the word "tens" in the first blank space (on the left) and "hundred" in the second.

The statement is now read as follows by the learners, "Ten tens equal one hundred."

This is the interpretation of the statement below the number (on the board) as applied to the places indicated by the arrows.

The next two consecutive places which we will consider (following tens and hundreds) are hundreds and thousands.

Proceeding similarly as above, have learners say, "Ten hundreds equal one thousand."

Similarly, elicit the following statements below from the learners.

1. "Ten thousands equal one ten-thousand."
2. "Ten ten-thousands equal one hundred-thousand."
3. "Ten hundred-thousands equal one million."
4. "Ten millions equal one ten-million."
5. "Ten ten-millions equal one hundred-million."
6. "Ten hundred-millions equal one billion."
7. "Ten billions equal one ten-billion."
8. "Ten ten-billions equal one hundred-billion."
9. "Ten hundred-billions equal one trillion."
10. "Ten trillions equal one ten-trillion."
11. "Ten ten-trillions equal one hundred-trillion."

Have each learner practice reciting from the ones' place on the right, all the way to the hundreds of trillions place on the left, as follows:

> "Ten ones equal one ten; ten tens equal one hundred; ten hundreds equal one thousand; ten thousands equal one ten-thousand"; and so on, up to "ten ten-trillions equal one hundred-trillion."

Have learners practice the recitations above to the level of facility; **then move on.**

Write the following on the board:

123,456,789,123,456

One ______ equals ten ______.

Tell the learners, "One of any unit, in one place of a whole number, equals ten units in the place to its right."

Draw arrows on the board pointing to the digits 5 and 6 at the right side of the number above.

Take your pointer, touch the 5 and ask, "What place is this?"

Learners respond, "Tens'."

Touch the 6 and ask, "What place is this?"

Learners respond, "Ones'."

Now have the learners focus on the statement on the board (with the blank spaces).

Tell them to place the word "ten" in the first blank space (on the left) and "ones" in the second.

The statement is now read as follows by the learners, "One ten equals ten ones."

This is the interpretation of the statement below the number (on the board), as applied to the places indicated by the arrows.

Erase the arrow pointing to the digit 6, and draw arrows pointing to the digits 4 and 5 (on the right side of the number).

Take your pointer, touch the 4 and ask, "What place is this?"

Learners respond, "Hundreds'."

Touch the 5 and ask, "What place is this?"

Learners respond, "Tens'."

Have learners focus on the statement on the board (with the blank spaces).

Tell them to place the word "hundred" in the first blank space (on the left), and "tens" in the second.

The statement is now read as follows by the learners, "One hundred equals ten tens."

This is the interpretation of the statement below the number (on the board), as applied to the places indicated by the arrows.

The next two consecutive places which we will consider (following hundreds and tens) are thousands and hundreds.

Proceeding similarly as above, have learners say, "One thousand equals ten hundreds."

Similarly, elicit the following statements from the learners:

1. "One ten-thousand equals ten thousands."
2. "One hundred-thousand equals ten ten-thousands."
3. "One million equals ten hundred-thousands."
4. "One ten-million equals ten millions."
5. "One hundred-million equals ten ten-millions."
6. "One billion equals ten hundred-millions."
7. "One ten-billion equals ten billions."
8. "One hundred-billion equals ten ten-billions."
9. "One trillion equals ten hundred-billions."
10. "One ten-trillion equals ten trillions."
11. "One hundred-trillion equals ten ten-trillions."

Have each learner practice reciting similarly, from the right end of the number, all the way to the left as follows:

> "One ten equals ten ones; one hundred equals ten tens; one thousand equals ten hundreds; one ten-thousand equals ten thousands"; and so on, up to "one hundred-trillion equals ten ten-trillions."

Have learners practice the recitations above to the level of facility; **then move on**.

PREPARING TO "TELL THE TRUTH" WHEN ADDING OR SUBTRACTING WITH WHOLE NUMBERS

Objectives: (a) Given numerals such as thirteen hundreds and eighteen ten-thousands, learners will rename them, as ten hundreds plus three hundreds, and ten ten-thousands plus eight ten-thousands, respectively.

(b) Learners will name the place value of any digit in a numeral up to the millions.

Place the following on the board:

By means of the diagrams above, have the learners see that
(a) fourteen tens equal ten tens plus four tens.
(b) eighteen hundreds equal ten hundreds plus eight hundreds.

Say, "Fourteen tens," to the learners, and have them reply, "Ten tens plus four tens."

Say, "Eighteen hundreds," to the learners, and have them reply, "Ten hundreds plus eight hundreds."

Ask,
"If I say, 'seventeen hundreds,' what do you say?" (Ten hundreds plus seven hundreds)
"If I say, 'nineteen tens,' what do you say?" (Ten tens plus nine tens)
"If I say, 'sixteen thousands,' what do you say?" (Ten thousands plus six thousands)
"If I say, 'thirteen thousands,' what do you say?" (Ten thousands plus three thousands)
"If I say, 'eleven hundreds,' what do you say?" (Ten hundreds plus one hundred)
"If I say, 'twelve thousands,' what do you say?" (Ten thousands plus two

thousands)

"If I say, 'sixteen ten-thousands,' what do you say?" (Ten ten-thousands plus six ten-thousands)

"If I say, 'nineteen hundred-thousands,' what do you say?" (Ten hundred-thousands plus nine hundred-thousands)

"If I say, 'fifteen ten-thousands,' what do you say?" (Ten ten-thousands plus five ten-thousands)

"If I say, 'seventeen hundred-thousands,' what do you say?" (Ten hundred-thousands plus seven hundred-thousands)

"If I say, 'fourteen millions,' what do you say?" (Ten millions plus four millions)

"If I say, 'nineteen hundred-millions,' what do you say?" (Ten hundred-millions plus nine hundred-millions)

"If I say, 'eighteen billions,' what do you say?" (Ten billions plus eight billions)

"If I say, 'fifteen ten-millions,' what do you say?" (Ten ten-millions plus five ten-millions)

"If I say, 'eleven hundred-billions,' what do you say?" (Ten hundred-billions plus one hundred-billion)

"If I say, 'twelve ten-billions,' what do you say?" (Ten ten-billions plus two ten-billions)

Read each example in Facility Exercises #89 (Workbook I) to the learners and have them reply in the same manner as above.

Have learners practice the exercises below to the level of facility; **then move on**.

To further prepare learners for the next section, return to "Place Value" and review the reading of large numerals.

Have them also practice telling the value of the digits in each numeral.

Write the following on the board:

6,384,795,102

Point to the 6 and ask, "What number does this digit represent?"

Tell learners, "Since this represents six billions, the digit 6 is in the billions' place."

Point to the 3 and ask, "What number does this digit represent?"

Tell learners, "Since this represents three hundred-millions, the digit 3 is in the hundred-millions' place."

Point to the 8 and ask, "What number does this digit represent?"

Tell learners, "Since this represents eighty millions, which means eight ten-millions, the digit 8 is in the ten-millions' place."

Point to the 4 and ask, "What number does this digit represent?"

Tell learners, "Since this represents four millions, the digit 4 is in the millions' place."

Ask the learners the following questions:

1. "The digit 7 is in what place?" (Hundred-thousands')
2. "The digit 9 is in what place?" (Ten-thousands')
3. "The digit 5 is in what place?" (Thousands')
4. "The digit 1 is in what place?" (Hundreds')
5. "The digit 0 is in what place?" (Tens')
6. "The digit 2 is in what place?" (Ones')

Ask the learners the same questions on each of the numbers below:

238,419,532,847,635
592,743,801,964
123,456,789
283,634
852
674,674,674,674,674
28,040,005,012
91,426,000
8,333

Write the following on the board:

8,473,972,048,160

Ask the following questions:

"Which digit is in the billions' place?" (3)
"Which digit is in the hundreds' place?" (1)
"Which digit is in the ten-thousands' place?" (4)
"Which digit is in the tens' place?" (6)
"Which digit is in the millions' place?" (2)
"Which digit is in the hundred-thousands' place?" (0)
"Which digit is in the thousands' place?" (8)
"Which digit is in the ones' place?" (0)
"Which digit is in the hundred-billions' place?" (4)
"Which digit is in the ten-millions' place?" (7)
"Which digit is in the trillions' place?" (8)
"Which digit is in the hundred-millions' place?" (9)
"Which digit is in the ten-billions' place?" (7)

Have learners practice the examples of Facility Exercises #90 (Workbook I) to the level of facility; **then move on**.

"TELLING THE TRUTH" WHEN ADDING WHOLE NUMBERS

Objective: The learners will tell the truth when adding any whole numbers, with regrouping, up to the hundreds of millions' place.

Write the following on the board:

```
  384,789,564
+ 789,759,679
```

In the ones' place, touch the 4 and the 9. Tell learners, "Add up the ones."

Learners must respond, "Thirteen ones."

Remind learners of the activity in the previous section: "If I say, 'thirteen ones', what do you say?"

Learners respond (as before), "Ten ones plus three ones."

Ask, "Where do we place the three ones?"

Based on their previous experience with adding whole numbers (with regrouping), learners should respond, "Under the nine ones."

Tell the learners to exchange the ten ones for one ten (like exchanging ten one-dollar bills for one ten-dollar bill), and take the one ten over to the place where the tens "live" (the tens' place).

Based on previous experience, learners will place the digit 1 (representing one ten) above the digit 6 in the tens' place.

In the tens' place, touch the 1, the 6, and the 7.

Tell learners, "Add up the tens."

Learners respond, "Fourteen tens."

Remind learners of the activity in the previous section: "If I say, 'fourteen tens', what do you say?"

Learners respond (as before), "Ten tens plus four tens."

Ask, "Where do we place the four tens?"

Based on their previous experience with adding whole numbers (with regrouping), learners should respond, "Under the seven tens."

Tell the learners to exchange the ten tens for one hundred (like exchanging ten ten-dollar bills for one hundred-dollar bill), and take the one hundred over to the place where the hundreds live (the hundreds' place).

Based on previous experience, learners will place the digit. 1 (representing one hundred) above the digit 5 in the hundreds' place.

In the hundreds' place, touch the 1, the 5, and the 6.

Tell learners, "Add up the hundreds."

Learners respond, "Twelve hundreds."

Remind learners of the activity in the previous section: "If I say, 'twelve hundreds', what do you say?"

Learners respond (as before), "Ten hundreds plus two hundreds."

Ask, "Where do we place the two hundreds?"

Based on their previous experience with adding whole numbers (with regrouping), learners should respond, "Under the six hundreds."

Tell the learners to exchange the ten hundreds for one thousand (like exchanging ten hundred-dollar bills for one thousand-dollar bill), and take the one thousand over to the place where the thousands live (the thousands' place).

Based on previous experience, learners will place the digit 1 (representing one thousand) above the digit 9, in the thousands' place.

In the thousands' place, touch the 1, the 9, and the 9.

Tell learners, "Add up the thousands."

Learners respond, "Nineteen thousands."

Remind learners of the activity in the previous section: "If I say, 'nineteen thousands', what do you say?"

Learners respond (as before), "Ten thousands plus nine thousands."

Ask, "Where do we place the nine thousands?"

Based on their previous experience with adding whole numbers (with regrouping), learners should respond, "Under the nine thousands."

Tell the learners to exchange the ten thousands for one ten-thousand (like exchanging ten thousand-dollar bills for one ten-thousand-dollar bill) and take the one ten-thousand over to the place where the ten-thousands live (the ten-thousands' place).

Based on previous experience, learners will place the digit 1 (representing one ten-thousand) above the digit 8 in the ten-thousands' place.

Proceeding similarly, elicit from learners that

1. there are fourteen ten-thousands.
2. fourteen ten-thousands equal ten ten-thousands plus four ten-thousands.
3. they must place four ten-thousands under the five ten-thousands.
4. they must exchange the ten ten-thousands for one hundred-thousand (like exchanging ten ten-thousand-dollar bills for one hundred-thousand-dollar bill).
5. they must take the one hundred-thousand over to the place where the hundred-thousands live (the hundred-thousands' place).

Continuing similarly, elicit from learners that

1. there are fifteen hundred-thousands.
2. fifteen hundred-thousands are equal to ten hundred-thousands plus five hundred-thousands.
3. they must place five hundred-thousands under the seven hundred-thousands.
4. they must exchange the ten hundred-thousands for one million (like exchanging ten hundred-thousand-dollar bills for one million-dollar bill).
5. they must take the one million over to the place where the millions live (the millions' place).

Similarly, elicit from learners that

1. there are fourteen millions.
2. fourteen millions equal ten millions plus four millions.
3. they must place four millions under the nine millions.
4. they must exchange ten millions for one ten-million (like exchanging ten million-dollar bills for one ten-million-dollar bill)
5. they must take the one ten-million over to the place where the ten-millions live (the ten-millions' place).

Similarly, elicit from learners that

1. there are seventeen ten-millions.
2. seventeen ten-millions equal ten ten-millions plus seven ten-millions.
3. they must place seven ten-millions under the eight ten-millions.
4. they must exchange ten ten-millions for one hundred-million (like exchanging ten ten-million-dollar bills for one hundred-million-dollar bill).
5. they must take the one hundred-million over to the place where the hundred-millions live (the hundred-millions' place).

Finally, elicit from learners that

1. there are eleven hundred-millions.
2. eleven hundred-millions equal ten hundred-millions plus one hundred-million.
3. they must place one hundred-million under the seven hundred-millions.
4. they must exchange the ten hundred-millions for one billion (like exchanging ten hundred-million-dollar bills for one billion-dollar bill).
5. they must take the one billion over to the billions' place and place it in the answer (since there are no other billions in the billions' place).

The board work finally looks like this:

```
   111 111 11
   384,789,564
+  789,759,679
 1,174,549,243
```

Have many learners go to the board, one at a time, and attempt (with your assistance) to go through the above articulation **with the same example** by themselves.

Each example in Facility Exercises #91 (Workbook I) is to be placed on the board, and discussed as above.

Have learners practice the examples of Facility Exercises #91 to the level of facility; **then move on**.

USING ADDITION TO SOLVE WORD PROBLEMS

Objective: The learners will apply addition skills to solving word problems.

Now that the learners can add any two whole numbers, we will provide some experience with problem solving based on this skill.

Write the following problem on the board:

> If you received 2 birthday cards on Wednesday and 3 on Thursday, how would you "figure out" the number of cards you had after two days?

Elicit from learners that they would add 2 to 3 and conclude that they received 5 cards over two days.

Write the following problem on the board:

> If a baseball team scores 3 runs in the first inning and 5 runs in the second, how can you figure out the amount of runs scored in two innings?

Elicit the answer to this question from the learners and have them conclude that 8 runs were scored in two innings.

Write the following problem on the board:

> If a basketball team scores 27 points in the first quarter and 35 points in the second, how can you figure out the number of points which have been scored in the first two quarters?

Elicit the answer to this question from the learners and have them conclude that 62 points were scored in two quarters.

Write the following problem on the board:

> If you are the owner of a toy store and you sell 3,738 toys during one week and 2,649 toys during the next week, how can you figure out how many toys you have sold in two weeks?

Elicit the answer to this question from the learners and have them conclude that

6,387 toys were sold in two weeks.

Write the following problem on the board:

If Mom buys a calculator for $178 and a computer for $469, how much money did she spend?

Elicit the answer to this problem from the learners.

Write the following problem on the board:

If one car costs $24,798, how would you figure out the cost of two cars?

Elicit from learners that they would add $24,798 to $24,798.

In Book II, they will use multiplication to solve this problem.

Have learners practice the examples of Facility Exercises #92 (Workbook I) to the level of facility; **then move on.**

"TELLING THE TRUTH" WHEN SUBTRACTING WITH WHOLE NUMBERS

Objective: The learners will tell the truth when subtracting one whole number from another, with exchange, up to the hundreds-of-millions' place.

Write the following on the board:

$$\begin{array}{r} 653{,}624{,}735 \\ -\ \underline{478{,}957{,}876} \end{array}$$

With your pointer in your hand, say to the learners, "Say what I touch."

Starting on the right of the problem, touch the 5, the minus sign, and the 6.

Learners say, "Five ones minus six ones."

Ask, "Can we take six ones from five ones?" (No)

Tell learners that they must

1. go "next door" to the tens' place, and take one ten from three tens, leaving two tens.
2. cross out the digit 3 in the tens' place, and write the digit 2 above it.
3. take the one ten and exchange it for ten ones (like exchanging one ten-dollar bill for ten one-dollar bills).
4. take the ten ones over to where the ones live (the ones' place), and add them to the five ones (making fifteen ones).
5. subtract the six ones from the fifteen ones, leaving nine ones.
6. write the nine ones under the six ones.

In the tens' place, touch the digit 2 (above the 3), the minus sign, and the 7.

Learners say, "Two tens minus seven tens."

Ask, "Can we take seven tens from two tens?" (No)

Tell learners that they must

1. go next door to the hundreds' place, and take one hundred from seven hundreds, leaving six hundreds.

2. cross out the digit 7 in the hundreds' place, and write the digit 6 above it.
3. take the one hundred and exchange it for ten tens (like exchanging one hundred-dollar bill for ten ten-dollar bills).
4. take the ten tens over to where the tens live (the tens' place), and add them to the two tens (making twelve tens).
5. subtract the seven tens from the twelve tens, leaving five tens.
6. write the five tens under the seven tens.

In the hundreds' place, touch the digit 6 (above the 7), the minus sign, and the 8.

Learners say, "Six hundreds minus eight hundreds."

Ask, "Can we take eight hundreds from six hundreds?" (No)

Tell learners that they must

1. go next door to the thousands' place, and take one thousand from the four thousands, leaving three thousands.
2. cross out the digit 4 in the thousands' place, and write the digit 3 above it.
3. take the one thousand and exchange it for ten hundreds (like exchanging one thousand-dollar bill for ten hundred-dollar bills).
4. take the ten hundreds over to where the hundreds live (the hundreds' place), and add them to the six hundreds (making sixteen hundreds).
5. subtract the eight hundreds from the sixteen hundreds, leaving eight hundreds.
6. write the eight hundreds under the eight hundreds.

Proceeding similarly, elicit from learners that since they cannot subtract seven thousands from three thousands, they must

1. take one ten-thousand from two ten-thousands, leaving one ten-thousand.
2. cross out the digit 2 and write the digit 1 above it.
3. exchange the one ten-thousand for ten thousands.
4. add the ten thousands to the three thousands (making thirteen thousands).
5. subtract the seven thousands from the thirteen thousands, leaving six thousands.
6. write the six thousands under the seven thousands.

Continuing similarly, elicit that since they cannot subtract five ten-thousands from one ten-thousand, they must

1. take one hundred-thousand from six hundred-thousands, leaving five hundred-thousands.
2. cross out the digit 6 and write the digit 5 above it.
3. exchange the one hundred-thousand for ten ten-thousands.
4. add the ten ten-thousands to the one ten-thousand (making eleven ten-thousands).

5. subtract the five ten-thousands from the eleven ten-thousands, leaving six ten-thousands.
6. write the six ten-thousands under the five ten-thousands.

Similarly, elicit that since they cannot subtract nine hundred-thousands from five hundred-thousands, they must

1. take one million from three millions, leaving two millions.
2. cross out the digit 3 and write the digit 2 above it.
3. exchange the one million for ten hundred-thousands.
4 add the ten hundred-thousands to the five hundred-thousands (making fifteen hundred-thousands).
5. subtract the nine hundred-thousands from the fifteen hundred-thousands, leaving six hundred-thousands.
6. write the six hundred-thousands under the nine hundred-thousands.

Similarly, elicit that since they cannot subtract eight millions from two millions, they must

1. take one ten-million from five ten-millions, leaving four ten-millions.
2. cross out the digit 5 and write the digit 4 above it.
3. exchange the one ten-million for ten millions.
4. add the ten millions to the two millions (making twelve millions).
5. subtract the eight millions from the twelve millions, leaving four millions.
6. write the four millions under the eight millions.

Similarly, elicit that since they cannot subtract seven ten-millions from four ten-millions, they must

1. take one hundred-million from six hundred-millions, leaving five hundred-millions.
2. cross out the digit 6 and write the digit 5 above it.
3. exchange the one hundred-million for ten ten-millions.
4. add the ten ten-millions to the four ten-millions (making fourteen ten-millions).
5 subtract the seven ten-millions from the fourteen ten-millions, leaving seven ten-millions.
6. write the seven ten-millions under the seven ten-millions.

Finally, we can take four hundred-millions from five hundred-millions, leaving one hundred-million.

Write one hundred-million under the four hundred-millions.

The board work finally looks like this:

$$
\begin{array}{ccccccccccc}
 & \scriptstyle 5 & \scriptstyle 14 & \scriptstyle 12 & \scriptstyle 15 & \scriptstyle 11 & \scriptstyle 13 & \scriptstyle 16 & \scriptstyle 12 & \\
 & \not{6} & \not{5} & \not{3}, & \not{6} & \not{2} & \not{4}, & \not{7} & \not{3} & {}^{1}5 \\
- & \underline{4} & \underline{7} & \underline{8,} & \underline{9} & \underline{5} & \underline{7,} & \underline{8} & \underline{7} & \underline{6} \\
 & 1 & 7 & 4, & 6 & 6 & 6, & 8 & 5 & 9
\end{array}
$$

Have many learners go to the board, one at a time, and attempt (with your assistance) to go through the above articulation with the **same example** by themselves.

Each example in Facility Exercises # 93 (Workbook I) is to be placed on the board and discussed as above.

Have learners practice the examples of Facility Exercises #93 to the level of facility; **then move on**.

Facility Exercises #94 through #97 provide mixed practice for the learners.

USING SUBTRACTION TO SOLVE WORD PROBLEMS

Objective: The learners will apply subtraction skills to solving word problems.

Now that learners can subtract any whole number from one which is larger, we will provide some experience with problem solving based on this skill.

Write the following problem on the board:

If you have $7 and you buy a ball for $2, how would you figure out how much money you have left?

Elicit from learners that they would subtract 2 from 7 and conclude that they had $5 left.

Write the following problem on the board:

Pretend you have 8 cents with some of it in your left pocket and the rest in your right pocket. If there are 5 cents in your left pocket, how would you figure out the amount of money in your right pocket?

Elicit from learners that they would subtract 5 from 8 and conclude that they had 3 cents in their right pockets.

Write the following problem on the board:

If there are 24 children in your class and 16 of them are girls, how would you figure out how many are boys?

Elicit from learners that they would subtract 16 from 24 and conclude that there were 8 boys.

Write the following on the board:

There are 403 girls in the Girl Scouts and 287 boys in the Boy Scouts. How would you figure out how many more girl scouts there are than boy scouts?

Elicit from learners that they would subtract 287 from 403 and conclude that there are 116 more girl scouts than boy scouts.

Write the following on the board:

> A large city had a population of 2,400,582. After 10 years, the population was 1,784,647. How would you figure out the loss in population over that period of time?

Elicit from learners that they would subtract 1,784,647 from 2,400,582 and conclude that there was a loss of 615,935 in the population over the 10 years.

Write the following on the board:

> Christine and her brother Ken inherited $81,428 from their uncle. If Christine's share of this money is $36,295, how would you figure out Ken's share?

Elicit from learners that they would subtract $36,295 from $81,428 and conclude that Ken's share is $45,133.

Have learners practice the examples of Facility Exercises #98 (Workbook I) to the level of facility; **then move on.**

FINDING THE MISSING NUMBER

Objective: Given an equation consisting of a sum or difference of two whole numbers equal to a third (whole number), and one of the three is missing, the learners will use the two numbers shown, to find the one which is missing.

The Facility Exercises in Workbook I, associated with this section, are designed to prepare learners for finding the missing numbers in equations which involve a single addition or subtraction sign.

Have learners practice the examples of Facility Exercises #99 (Workbook I) to the level of facility; **then move on**.

Prepare copies of the examples below for your learners. Elicit from them the missing number in each one.

3 + 2 = ___	6 = ___ + 5	___ = 8 − 5
3 = 6 − ___	5 + ___ = 10	9 = 3 + ___
___ − 3 = 1	___ = 9 − 2	___ + 7 = 9
9 = ___ + 4	4 − ___ = 2	3 = ___ − 7
___ = 4 + 3	___ = 7 − 1	___ − 1 = 1
8 − ___ = 4	7 + ___ = 10	10 = 4 + ___
5 = 9 − ___	7 − 4 = ___	___ = 2 + 2
8 + 2 = ___	8 = ___ − 2	1 = ___ − 4

Given the example, 3 + 2 = _____, you may elicit the answer by asking, "Three plus two equals a certain number. What is that number?"

Given the example, 3 = 6 − _____, you may elicit the answer by asking, "If you take a certain number from six, the answer is three. What is that number?"

Given the example, _____ - 3 = 1, you may elicit the answer by asking, "If you take three from a certain number, the answer is one. What is that number?"

Have learners note that three numbers are involved in each example above.

In the first problem, the three numbers are 3, 2, and 5.

Let us call each set of three numbers a triple.

Have learners say each triple in the remaining examples above, while writing them down.

Eventually, they should have written the following:

3,2,5	6,1,5	3,8,5
3,6,3	5,5,10	9,3,6
4,3,1	7,9,2	2,7,9
9,5,4	4,2,2	3,10,7
7,4,3	6,7,1	2,1,1
8,4,4	7,3,10	10,4,6
5,9,4	7,4,3	4,2,2
8,2,10	8,10,2	1,5,4

Have learners pay attention to the following:

1. Each triple has two smaller numbers and one which is largest.
2. When we add the two smaller numbers, the result is the largest number in that triple.
3. When we subtract one of the smaller numbers from the largest, the result is the other smaller number.
4. Each example with a plus symbol on one side of the equal sign, has the largest number (of the three) on the other side of the equal sign.
5. Each example with a minus symbol has the largest number on the left of the minus.

Let us look at the first example above:

3 + 2 = ____

"Which number of the triple is missing?" (The largest)
"How do you know the largest is the missing number?" (Because there is a plus symbol on one side of the equal sign, the largest number of the triple is on the other side, and it's missing)
"Which two numbers of the triple are shown?" (The two smaller numbers)
"How can you use the two numbers shown to find the one which is missing?" (Add the two smaller numbers, 3 and 2)
"Why do you add?" (When you add the two smaller numbers, the result is the largest)
"So what is the missing number?" (5)

Let us look at the second example above:

$$3 = 6 - \_\_\_\_$$

"Which number of the triple is missing?" (One of the smaller numbers)
"How do you know a smaller number is missing?" (Because the number 6 is on the left of the minus sign, it is the largest; so the missing number is one of the smaller numbers)
"Which two numbers of the triple are shown?" (The largest and one of the smaller numbers)
"How can you use the numbers shown to find the one which is missing?" (Subtract the smaller number from the largest)
"Why do you subtract?" (When you subtract the smaller from the largest, the result is the other smaller number)
"So what is the missing number?" (3)

Let us look at the third example above:

$$\_\_\_\_ - 3 = 1$$

"Which number of the triple is missing?" (The largest)
"How do you know the largest is missing?" (Because the number on the left of the minus sign is the largest and it is missing)
"Which two numbers of the triple are shown?" (The two smaller numbers)
"How can you use the numbers shown to find the one which is missing?" (Add them)
"Why do you add?" (When you add the two smaller numbers, the result is the largest)
"So what is the missing number?" (4)

Let us look at the fourth example above:

$$9 = \_\_\_\_ + 4$$

"Which number of the triple is missing?" (One of the smaller numbers)
"How do you know a smaller number is missing?" (Because there is a plus symbol on one side of the equal sign, the largest is on the other side, and it is shown; so one of the smaller numbers is missing)
"Which two numbers of the triple are shown?" (The largest and one of the smaller numbers)
"How can you use the numbers shown to find the one which is missing?" (Subtract the smaller number from the largest)
"Why do you subtract?" (When you subtract a smaller from the largest, the result is the other smaller number)
"So what is the missing number?" (5)

Repeat the above types of questions for each of the remaining examples.

After much practice, learners will know

1. where to locate the largest number of a triple in an equation involving one plus or minus sign.
2. how to use the two numbers shown to find the one which is missing.

Have learners write the following example:

$$41 = 18 + \underline{\qquad}$$

Ask the following questions:
"Which two numbers of the triple are shown?"
"How will you use the two numbers shown to find the one which is missing?"

Have learners do the work to find the answer (see below).

$$\begin{array}{r} 41 \\ -\underline{18} \\ 23 \end{array}$$

Tell learners, "So the missing number is twenty-three."

Have learners check the answer to 41 = 18 + ____ by asking, "Is it really true that forty-one equals eighteen plus twenty-three?"

Have learners write the following example:

$$542 = \underline{\qquad} - 184$$

Ask the following questions:
"Which two numbers of the triple are shown?"
"How will you use the two numbers shown to find the one which is missing?"

Have learners do the work to find the answer (see below).

$$\begin{array}{r} 542 \\ +\underline{184} \\ 726 \end{array}$$

"So the missing number is seven hundred twenty-six."

Have learners check the answer to 542 = ____ − 184 by asking, "Is it really true that five hundred forty-two equals seven hundred twenty-six minus one hundred eighty-four?"

Have learners write the following example:

$$831 - \underline{\qquad} = 152$$

Ask the following questions:
"Which two numbers of the triple are shown?"
"How will you use the two numbers shown to find the one which is missing?"

Have learners do the work to find the answer (see below).

$$\begin{array}{r} 831 \\ -\underline{152} \\ 679 \end{array}$$

Tell learners, "So the missing number is six hundred seventy-nine."

Have learners check the answer to 831 – _____ = 152 by asking, "Is it really true that eight hundred thirty-one minus six hundred seventy-nine equals one hundred fifty-two?"

Lead learners through the examples of Facility Exercises #100 (Workbook I) by means of the questions above.

Have them practice the examples of Facility Exercises #100 to the level of facility; **then move on.**

In this section, a more concise procedure for finding the missing number is presented.

Have learners go through the following steps for every example in Facility Exercises #101 (Workbook I).

1. Look at the sign.
2. Let the sign "tell you" where the largest number is situated.
3. Look where the largest number is supposed to be situated; either it is missing or it is shown.
4. "Largest number missing" triggers add (add the two numbers which are shown).
5. "Largest number shown" triggers subtract (subtract the smaller from the larger).

Have learners practice the examples of Facility Exercises #101 to the level of facility; **then move on.**

MENTAL ADDITION

Objective: The learners will respond quickly and accurately to such examples, presented orally, as
(a) 20 + 17, 60 + 14 and 40 + 12; and
(b) 36 + 8, 65 + 3 and 83 + 9.

Place the following diagram on the board:

Tell learners to imagine that 10 is written above each blank space.

Point to the blank on the left, the plus sign and the next blank.

Have learners say, "Ten plus ten, twenty."

Point to the next plus sign and blank.

Have learners say, "Plus ten, thirty."

Point to the next plus sign and blank.

Have learners say, "Plus ten, forty."

Continue similarly while learners say, "Plus ten, fifty; plus ten, sixty," and so on, up to "plus ten, one hundred."

Repeat this exercise as often as necessary for learners to recite the above fluently and **without looking at the diagram** on the board.

Now tell learners to imagine that 9 is written above the blank on the left and 10 is written above the others.

Point to the blank on the left, the plus sign and the next blank.

Have learners say, "Nine plus ten, nineteen."

Point to the next plus sign and blank.

Have learners say, "Plus ten, twenty-nine."

Continue similarly up to "plus ten, ninety-nine."

Repeat this exercise as often as necessary for learners to recite the above fluently and without looking at the diagram on the board.

By having learners imagine that 8 (or 7, 6, 5, 4, 3, 2, 1) is written above the blank on the left and 10 is written above the others, they will learn to count by tens, starting from 8 (or 7, 6, 5, 4, 3, 2, 1), up to 98 (or 97, 96, 95, 94, 93, 92, 91).

Have learners practice the above **orally** to the level of facility; **then move on**.

Tell learners to start from 10 and count by tens to 100.

Ask, "If we start from 10 and count by tens to 100, what comes after 20? After 50? After 80? After 30? After 60? After 10? After 40? After 70?"

Be sure learners see that by adding 10 to 30, for example, we get the number "after" 30 (when we count by tens to 100).

Ask, "What is 20 plus 10?" (Thirty, since 30 "comes after" 20 when we count by tens to 100) "What is 50 plus 10? 80 plus 10? 30 plus 10? 60 plus 10? 10 plus 10? 40 plus l0? 70 plus l0?"

Remind learners that "teen" is another name for ten.

Ask many questions such as:
"Teen makes 20 jump to ____ ?" (Thirty)
"Teen makes 70 jump to ____ ?"

Now write the following on the board:

50 + 3

Ask, "What's 50 plus 3?"

Ask the following questions:

"What's 70 plus 4?"
"What's 40 plus 5?"
"What's 80 plus 2?"
"What's 30 plus 7?"
"What's 50 plus 6?"
"What's 10 plus 8?"

Write the following on the board:
60 + 4
60 + 14

Ask the following questions:
"What's 60 plus 4?"
"So what's 60 plus 14?"

Be sure learners see the following:

```
 60  +  14
 /      |\
sixty  teen four
```

Have learners see that teen makes sixty jump to seventy and we must add the 4.

Tell learners, "Sixty plus 4 equals 64; so 60 plus 14 equals 74."

Give learners much practice in **looking** at examples such as 20 + 14 and 50 + 19; then giving the answers **orally**.

After learners have facility on the visual level, **ask** many questions such as:
"What is 30 plus 6? So, what is 30 plus 16?"
"What is 20 plus 5? So, what is 20 plus 15?"
"What is 50 plus 1? So, what is 50 plus 11?"
"What is 40 plus 2? So, what is 40 plus 12?"
"What is 10 plus 18?"
"What is 60 plus 7?"
"What is 70 plus 19?"
"What is 20 plus 4?"
"What is 80 plus 12?"
"What is 40 plus 3?"
"What is 60 plus 15?"

Please note: the above questioning is **oral**, not visual.

Emphasize that "teen" (if there is a teen) makes the "tens part" of the example "jump."

Keep **asking** such questions, until learners answer with facility.

Write the following on the board:

5 + 3
25 + 3
75 + 3
45 + 3
85 + 3

Ask the following questions:
"What is 5 plus 3?"
"So what is 25 plus 3? 75 plus 3? 45 plus 3? 85 plus 3?"
"What is 7 plus 2?"

"So what is 37 plus 2? 97 plus 2? 67 plus 2? 17 plus 2?"
"What is 4 plus 4?"
"So what is 34 plus 4? 44 plus 4? 94 plus 4? 74 plus 4?"
"What is 2 plus 5?"
"So what is 32 plus 5? 72 plus 5? 82 plus 5? 22 plus 5?"

Ask many similar questions until learners answer with facility.

Write the following on the board:

8 + 7

38 + 7
68 + 7
58 + 7
78 + 7

28 + 7
18 + 7
48 + 7
88 + 7

Ask, "What is 8 plus 7?"

Demonstrate the following on the board:

38 + 7

30 + 15

Ask,
"When you look at 38 + 7, can you 'see' 30 + 15?"
"So what is 38 + 7?" (45)

Write the following on the board:

68 + 7

Ask,
"Look at 68 + 7. Can you see 60 + 15 in 68 + 7?"
"So what is 68 + 7?"

"In order to add 58 + 7, what should you think first?" (50 + 15)
"So what is 58 + 7?"

"In order to add 78 + 7, what should you think first?"
"So what is 78 + 7?"

"What is 28 + 7? 18 + 7? 48 + 7? 88 + 7?"

Write the following on the board:

5 + 8

75 + 8
35 + 8
15 + 8
55 + 8

45 + 8
25 + 8
65 + 8
85 + 8

By asking similar questions, elicit answers to the above sums.

Repeat this activity with different sets of sums such as 7 + 7, 27 + 7, 87 + 7, and so on.

When learners have acquired facility at this level, move on to the next.

Write the following on the board:

6 + 8

36 + 8	16 + 8
76 + 8	86 + 8
26 + 8	46 + 8
56 + 8	66 + 8

Ask,
"Six plus eight?"
"So thirty-six plus eight?"
"So seventy-six plus eight?"
"So twenty-six plus eight?"
"So fifty-six plus eight?"
"So sixteen plus eight?"
"So eighty-six plus eight?"
"So forty-six plus eight?"
"So sixty-six plus eight?"

Repeat this activity with different sets of sums such as 7 + 9, 27 + 9, 87 + 9, and so on.

Ask,
"When I say, 'Twenty-nine plus eight,' can you hear 'twenty plus seventeen'?"
"So what is 29 + 8?"

Say the following to learners, and ask what they hear in each case, before answering the question:
"Forty-eight plus eight." (Forty plus sixteen)
"So forty-eight plus eight equals _____?" (Fifty-six)
"Sixty-six plus nine." (Sixty plus fifteen)
"So sixty-six plus nine equals _____?" (Seventy-five)
"Seventy-four plus six." (Seventy plus ten)
"So seventy-four plus six equals _____?" (Eighty)
"Twenty-nine plus seven."
"So twenty-nine plus seven equals _____?"
"Twenty-seven plus nine."
"So twenty-seven plus nine equals _____?"
"Thirty-nine plus three."
"So thirty-nine plus three equals _____?"

"Eighty-four plus seven."
"So eighty-four plus seven equals _____?"
"Seventeen plus eight." (Ten plus fifteen)
"So seventeen plus eight equals _____?"
"Thirty-six plus six."
"So thirty-six plus six equals _____?"

Ask many similar questions until learners answer with facility.

Now ask the following questions:
"What is 26 + 5?"
"What is 39 + 2?"
"What is 54 + 8?"
"What is 86 + 7?"
"What is 49 + 4?"

Ask many similar questions until learners answer with facility.

Ask,
"What is 40 + 30?"
"What is 8 + 6?"
"So when I say, 'Forty-eight plus thirty-six,' can you hear 'seventy plus fourteen'?"
"So what is 48 + 36?"
"What is 46 + 38?"

Ask,
"What is 20 + 60?"
"What is 8 + 9?"
"So when I say, 'Twenty-eight plus sixty-nine,' can you hear 'eighty plus seventeen'?"
"So what is 28 + 69?"
"What is 29 + 68?"

Ask,
"When I say, 'Fifty-eight plus twenty-five,' do you hear seventy plus thirteen?"
"So what is fifty-eight plus twenty-five?" (Eighty-three)

Say the following to learners and ask what they hear in each case.
"Sixty-seven plus twenty-seven." (Eighty plus fourteen)
"So sixty-seven plus twenty-seven equals _____?"
"Thirty-nine plus thirty-seven." (Sixty plus sixteen)
"So thirty-nine plus thirty-seven equals _____?"
"Forty-five plus thirty-nine." (Seventy plus fourteen)
"So forty-five plus thirty-nine equals _____?"
"Seventy-six plus nineteen." (Eighty plus fifteen)

"So seventy-six plus nineteen equals _____?"
"Twenty-six plus fifty-six." (Seventy plus twelve)
"So twenty-six plus fifty-six equals _____?"
"Fifty-eight plus eighteen." (Sixty plus sixteen)
"So fifty-eight plus eighteen equals _____?"
"Forty-seven plus forty-four." (Eighty plus eleven)
"So forty-seven plus forty-four equals _____?"
"Sixteen plus eighteen." (Twenty plus fourteen)
"So sixteen plus eighteen equals _____?"

Ask many similar questions until learners answer with facility.

Now ask the following questions:
"What is 47 plus 36?"
"What is 54 plus 43?"
"What is 29 plus 39?"
"What is 82 plus 17?"
"What is 28 plus 28?"
"What is 36 plus 36?"
"What is 18 plus 18?"
"What is 16 plus 16?"
"What is 45 plus 24?"
"What is 27 plus 27?"
"What is 32 plus 32?"
"What is 38 plus 58?"

Ask many similar questions until learners answer with facility.

The **Professor B Math Charts #8 and #9** are used by teachers to play exciting, rapid-response games.

These games encourage learners to cognitively process the thinking strategies described in this section as rapidly as possible.

COLUMN ADDITION

Objective: The learners will add more than two whole numbers.

Write the following on the board:

$$\begin{array}{r} 6 \\ 8 \\ 9 \\ 5 \\ 7 \\ 6 \\ 5 \\ 7 \\ 3 \\ +\,\underline{6} \end{array}$$

Lead learners through the above addition as follows:
"Six plus 8?" (Fourteen)
"Plus 9?" (Twenty-three)
"Plus 5?" (Twenty-eight)
"Plus 7?" (Thirty-five)
"Plus 6?" (Forty-one)
"Plus 5?" (Forty-six)
"Plus 7?" (Fifty-three)
"Plus 3?" (Fifty-six)
"Plus 6?" (Sixty-two)
"The answer is 62."

Write the following on the board:

6	7	3	1	9	5
5	3	8	2	8	9
8	5	4	3	7	4
4	8	9	4	3	7
9	9	5	5	4	3
5	6	3	6	5	9
8	7	6	7	6	8
7	8	7	8	7	4
4	4	5	9	6	6
+ 8	+ 5	8	+ 6	+ 8	7
		9			5
		7			9
		+ 8			+ 8

Lead learners through the above additions as was done for the first example.

Write the following on the board:

5
9
7
8
6
8
4
+ 7

Now lead learners through the above example as follows:

"Add 5 + 9 and hold the answer in your mind. Hold it 'real tight' and do not say it out loud."

"Now add 7 to the number in your mind and hold that real tight. Do not say it out loud."

"Add 8 to the number in your mind and hold that real tight. Do not say it out loud."

"Add 6 to the number in your mind and hold that real tight. Do not say it out loud."

"Add 8 to the number in your mind and hold that real tight. Do not say it out loud."

"Add 4 to the number in your mind and hold that real tight. Do not say it out loud."

"Add 7 to the number in your mind and hold that real tight."

Ask various learners, "What number are you holding now?"

Lead learners through many column additions in the above manner.

Have learners practice the examples of Facility Exercises #102 (Workbook I) to the level of facility; **then move on**.

Write the following on the board:

```
   678
   567
   869
   756
   877
   498
 + 345
```

Lead learners through the addition of the right column, holding the partial sums in their minds as they go.

Tell learners, "The sum of the first column is 50. Put down the zero and 'carry' the 5." (Learners should write a small 5 on top of the middle column)

Lead learners through the addition of the middle column (including the 5 which was carried over), holding the partial sums in their minds as they go.

Tell learners, "The sum of the middle column is 49. Put down the 9 and carry the 4." (Learners should write a small 4 on top of the left column)

Lead learners through the addition of the left column (including the 4 which was carried over), holding the partial sums in their minds as they go.

Tell learners,
"The sum of the left column is 45."
"Write down the 45."

Have learners read the answer.
"Four thousand, five hundred ninety."

Write the following on the board:

```
   303,412
       309
     5,785
   123,456
     6,740
         3
        26
    45,694
       236
 +      17
```

Lead learners through this example in a manner similar to the above.

You may allow individual learners to recite the additions in the various columns independently.

Have learners practice the examples of Facility Exercises # 103 (Workbook I) to the level of facility; **then move on.**

The next set of exercises provides mixed practice on word problems which require addition, subtraction, column addition, or a combination of these operations.

Have learners practice the examples of Facility Exercises #104 (Workbook I) to the level of facility; **then move on to Book Two**.